YOUR POCKET GUIDE TO SEX

NICK FISHER

PENGUIN BOOKS

Introduction to the Penguin Edition

Writing a book is never easy. But it is only work. You get up early, stay up late; you bite your fingernails and you stare at a computer screen until your eyes go squinty. Fair enough.

Getting published is another ball game.

Your Pocket Guide to Sex is my fourth book. I was asked to write it for the Health Education Authority. They knew what they wanted: a book for the 16–25 age group, something spunky and punchy that would grab the reader, something full of facts and information; something with advice about safe sex. It had to be sexy, unpatronizing and, most of all, it had to be done *fast*. There were urgent deadlines to meet. Fair enough.

So, it was goodbye, fingernails – hello, squint.

Within a few weeks I get to enjoy pats on the back, as I grin inanely for promotional photographs under a big advertising banner at the London Bookfair in Earls Court.

Job well done. Cheque in the post. Lovely jubbly.

Two days later I come home at night to find a curious message from the HEA on my answerphone, telling me the government has banned the sale of the very same book. The next day brought newspapers proclaiming that the text was a lurid sex guide full of 'distasteful smut and pornography'. They also wrongly stated that it was written for children.

Suddenly, I'm a chief smut-monger and state pornographer. I've gone from being a jobbing writer to being a 'controversial freelance journalist'; my mum gets doorstepped by tabloid news hounds; and my answerphone clocks up seventy-one messages in twenty-four hours.

It's a 'Sex Storm', said one sad paper, as I drowned under a wave of moral madness. Everyone and their dog, from politicians to TV celebs, chipped in their two bob's worth. Some said the language was disgusting; others felt that mention of oral and homosexual sex made the whole thing tantamount to the devil's own handiwork.

Meanwhile, most sex-education professionals able to get hold of a copy said it was very effective and long overdue.

No one, of course, asked what anyone between the ages of 16 and 25 thought. Which is a pity, because that's who *Your Pocket Guide to Sex* is for.

This is a book for young adults who want to know more about sex: this is *not* a book for government ministers who think young people already know too much.

CONTENTS

INTRODUCTION

Maybe you're already having sex which is perfect. It might be so toe-curlingly, back-archingly brilliant, that you just haven't got time to read this book. Fair enough. Good on you.

But most of us aren't having perfect sex. Most of us have got questions we'd like to ask or problems we'd like to share, but are reticent, because we don't know what's acceptable. Or we're just plain embarrassed.

Your pocket guide to sex tries to prod around in the areas people have difficulty with. It tries to explain a range of facts, explode a bundle of myths, give useful contacts, describe what safer sex is and even dig up a laugh or two's worth of sexual trivia.

There are quotes from people who've 'been there and done that', there are comments from seasoned celebrities and there's even some assorted nonsense about what we used to think, do and feel about sex in Ancient Times.

There are lots of things we didn't include. For example, there's no 'A-Z of 101 new sexual positions to bonk your beloved'. There's no devilishly intricate technical stuff about 'how to achieve a mass of multiple orgasms during the commercial break'.

So beware, this isn't a book for sexual anoraks. This is no part-work guide to better loving, more Brownie points and a bigger dick. This is a book about getting to know yourself, your partners and safely enjoying and experimenting with the sex that you do have.

So what if you come too quickly, can't get orgasms or are unsure about undressing in front of someone else? So what if you've never had sex and don't know where to start? Maybe you're a lot more like the rest of us than you think.

With a bit of luck, **Your pocket guide to sex** might help you understand the complexities of sex, be aware of the dangers, feel more confident in yourself and realise that good relations and emotions, can count for a lot more than notches on the bed post.

Good sex is about quality not quantity.

Chapter 1

Sexuality

66 There's this illusion
that homosexuals
have sex and
heterosexuals fall in
love. That's
completely untrue.
Everybody wants to
be loved. 99

Boy George

HUMAN BEINGS ARE SEXUAL ANIMALS

No matter how sophisticated and developed we've become, we're still enormously motivated by the primeval instinct to perform sex. And, we've discovered that sex is not only necessary to continue the species, it also feels good too. Whether it's right or wrong, sex has become an important and powerful part of our society.

Sexuality is the state or quality of being sexual. To some degree we define ourselves by our sexual orientation. You can be heterosexual – you're attracted to the opposite sex. Or you could be homosexual – you're attracted to your own sex. Or bisexual – you're attracted to both sexes.

It's all perfectly natural. As in all areas of human activity, people want to make rules about sexuality. The truth is, there are no rules.

Puberty problems

Our sexuality develops from a very early age, but only tends to become obvious in adolescence when

"Recently I got involved in a gay thing with a boy I had known for ages. All we did was kiss and fondle. Now I'm scared my girlfriend will find out as she's good friends with the boy involved. I still love her, but I couldn't help my feelings for him."
(17 year old male)

hormonal changes at puberty start to set off sexual impulses and feelings.

Sometimes the feelings can be disturbing if they aren't what is perceived to be 'normal'.

Feeling guilty for feeling

Because we live in a predominantly heterosexual society, the pressure exists for people to conform. That means there's a risk that homosexual feelings get thought of as wrong or abnormal, which is very hard if you're the one doing the feeling.

But some people are perfectly at ease with what they feel:

> *"I realised I was gay when I was 10. Only my mum knows that I am gay. We don't talk about it at all. I know she is upset, but I'm happy to be gay. I'm just a normal run of the mill guy, who does everything other guys do, except I don't have any interest in girls."*
> (19 year old male)

Feeling guilty for not feeling

Some people feel strong sexual urges from an early age, whether they're homosexual or heterosexual urges. But others might feel nothing. Because sex is made into such a major deal in our society, some people get to feel guilty because they feel so little.

> *"Sometimes I feel like a freak because I'm not talking about sex all the time. I'm just not that interested. Of course I'd like a boyfriend and I do like sex. But sex isn't the most important thing in the Universe!"*
> (22 year old female)

Celibacy

Just because we're sexual beings doesn't mean we have to turn sex into a full-time obsession. Some people actively prefer to be celibate, and live without sex. They choose not to complicate their lives, believing that there are better ways to use their time and emotion.

> *"Celibacy is a singular source of spiritual fertility in the world."*
> Pope John Paul II (1992)

And also, there are those people who don't enjoy or get that excited by sex and are happy to let it just be a very small part of their life.

> *"I've been celibate for 14 years...I wouldn't wish my great wobbly body on top of anybody else's."*
> Stephen Fry

> *"Sex is fine. But sometimes I'd much rather just have a nice cup of tea and a chat."*
> Boy George

HETEROSEXUALITY

Depending on which survey you read, some state that 10 per cent of the population are homosexual and 90 per cent are heterosexual. Others maintain that 10 per cent are homosexual, only 60 per cent are truly heterosexual, and the other 30 per cent are bisexual. Who knows?

Although heterosexuality is socially accepted as being the sexuality enjoyed by the majority, the name comes from the Greek word meaning 'other' or 'different'. People who are heterosexual are attracted to the opposite sex.

The advantage, or as some would see it, the disadvantage of wanting to have sex with members of the opposite sex, is that pregnancy is a frequent side effect.

Only heterosexual couples can get married under the Christian church, so basically, it's the only form of sexuality which gets the full and unquestionable stamp of approval.

> *"Marriage is a social device for regulating heterosexual activity, preventing socially disruptive competition and establishing the mutually advantageous responsibilities of the spouses and their offspring."*
> Institute for Sex Research

It's true that society and the law make it easier to be heterosexual than homosexual or bisexual. But of course, that doesn't make heterosexuality the 'right' way. It's simply the most common form of sexuality.

HOMOSEXUALITY

The dictionary definition of a homosexual is 'a person who is sexually attracted to members of the same sex'. Both men and women can be homosexual (or 'gay'), although some gay women prefer to be called lesbians.

Various studies claim that up to 10 per cent of the population is homosexual.

Some people know that they're homosexual from a very early age and are perfectly comfortable in that knowledge. Whereas others repress their feelings, sometimes all of their lives, because they're scared and even ashamed of being different.

"I was married for 21 years. Happily married really. Then I met my lover. Within six months I'd left my husband and was living with this woman. I don't know if I was gay all those years. But I know I am now."
(44 year old woman)

There are controversial studies being carried out to try and determine what makes people homosexual as opposed to heterosexual.

The truth is no one really knows.

Sex practices

Some homosexual men have anal sex, but not all by any means. (Some heterosexuals, men and women, also enjoy anal sex.) Some homosexuals enjoy mutual masturbation, oral sex or 'rimming', (the practise of tonguing around the anus). Lesbians, too, might enjoy oral sex or finger fucking or sex with vibrators – the same as some heterosexuals.

But to define sexuality purely by what sex acts you get up to is very shortsighted. Sexuality is as much about emotion as it is about sex.

"There's this illusion that homosexuals have sex and heterosexuals fall in love. That's completely untrue. Everybody wants to be loved."
Boy George

And most sexual practices are practically the same. They usually involve sensual touch, excitement and affection, no matter what your sexuality.

Homosexuality and history

Homosexuality is increasingly accepted and understood in our society, but that's not always been the case. The laws against 'sodomy', which is another name for anal sex, date back to the Emperor Justinian (483–562 AD) who thought that this particular sexual act was the main cause of major earthquakes.

King Henry VIII was dead set against 'buggery' and was responsible for implementing the first law prohibiting the act in 1533.

By 1956, things hadn't got much better when section 12 of the Sexual Offences Act stated that it 'is a felony to commit buggery with another person or with an animal'.

Thankfully, since then, the law against homosexual sex has lightened up a fair bit. And in 1967 it was made legal for consenting men over the age of 21 to partake of 'homosexual activity' in private.

Lesbianism

The history of lesbianism has been much lower key. There is one story told that in the 19th century parliament were all set to bring in legislation against lesbian acts, but they never happened because Queen Victoria refused to believe that such things ever took place.

So while men got all the flack for their homosexual acts and had various damning laws against them, lesbians got left alone. They lived not so much outside the law as beneath it.

One theory is, that because lesbian sex doesn't involve a penis, then it isn't 'real' sex. So then it's not worth getting in a flap about. Needless to say this sort of theory is always thought up by men!

Homophobia

Homophobia is a term used to describe the hostile attitudes that some sections of society have against homosexuals.

Homophobia, or the fear of homosexuality, is responsible for horrible crimes like 'queer bashing' where men attack homosexuals purely for being who they are.

A lot of the slang that has evolved to describe homosexuals is insulting and derogatory (poof, pansy, bum bandit, etc). In fact, it's used by heterosexual men to insult each other too. As though the ultimate insult one 'straight' man can make to another is to accuse him of being homosexual.

Men are thought to be generally more homophobic than women. But in the same way that male institutions are thought to be breeding grounds for homophobia, some girls experienced the same at boarding school.

> *"I remember one time I scratched this girl's back in the middle of the night I was, you know, nine and she was twelve and she asked me to scratch her back. A nun ran in, ripped me off her back, threw me against the lockers, beat the shit out of me and called me a lesbian. I didn't know what a lesbian was."*
> Cyndi Lauper
> on her school days.

BISEXUALITY

Casanova was bisexual

A bisexual is someone who feel sexual attraction to both sexes. And for many people this is perfectly natural.

Sexuality is an everchanging thing. At certain points in their life, people may be attracted to either one sex or the other. Others may fancy both sexes all the time.

Some people are quite scared of being in any way sexually different, so they've got elaborate ways of repressing any conflicting sexual feelings they might have.

> *"My feeling is that we are all bisexual. I don't believe there is anyone who could honestly say at some point in their lives they have not been attracted to a member of the same sex."*
> Ken Livingstone MP

One of the areas that seems to give humans major problems is defining their sexuality. We want everything to be clear cut and precise. But the truth is that the world is not carved up into two types of person: heterosexual and homosexual. We're more complex than that. If only we could accept and not care that sometimes we don't know what we are, then life and sex might get a lot simpler. There was an innovative study written in the late 1940s that puts it very clearly.

As Alfred Kinsey said in his report *Sexual Behaviour in the Human Male:* "Not all things are black, nor all white, for nature rarely deals with discreet categories. Only the human mind invents categories and tries to force facts into separate pigeon holes. The living world is a continuum in each and every one of it's aspects. The sooner we learn this concerning human sexual behaviour, the sooner we shall reach a sound understanding of the realities of sex."

"I've slept with women and I love it."
Neneh Cherry

"I am a practising heterosexual ... but bisexuality immediately doubles your chances for a date on a Saturday night."
Woody Allen

Chapter 2

Your body

> **"** How can you expect your lover to know what turns you on if you don't know yourself? **"**
>
> *25 year old female*

GETTING TO KNOW YOUR BODY – WOMEN

Just because you were born with your body and have lived with it for umpteen years, doesn't necessarily mean that you know everything about it. When it comes to their sex organs, a lot of people know very little, often because they've been brought up thinking that fiddling, prodding or investigating 'down below' is 'dirty'.

For women, Nature makes it even more difficult to get to know your love tackle because it's all been carefully tucked away and disguised by a mound of hair.

The simplest thing to do to get a proper handle on what's what, is to shut the bathroom door, take a mirror and have a good old gander.

The view...

The outermost part of a woman's sex organs is her vulva. This external area protects the opening to the vagina and the urethra, (which is the tube urine passes through). Two folds of skin that meet in a peak are the outer vaginal lips or labia majora. These are made quite plump to act as a cushion during sex.

One labia is often noticeably larger than the other.

Inside these are the labia minora which are the thinner more sensitive lips which join to form the clitoral hood; a loose lip of skin that covers the clitoris.

The clitoris is where it all happens. It's the most sensitive area of a woman's sexual organs. And its name comes from the Greek word meaning 'key'.

The clitoris is actually remarkably like a man's penis in its construction. It has a flexible shaft and hood which swell with blood during sex, with a head that gets hard and phenomenally sensitive just before orgasm.

Yet considering the similarity between the penis and the clitoris, it's surprising the number of men who can't find the clitoris and haven't got much of a clue what to do with it even if they did. So the best thing, if you've got a clitoris of your own, is to check it out intimately for yourself. Then you can always show a lover exactly what happens down there, what feels best and how you like it done.

One of the big problems with the clitoris is that it's very well disguised and most of what it's about is completely hidden from view. The clitoris is like an iceberg; you only see the tip of what's going on. Beneath the skin is a complex network of valves, ducts and spongy tissue.

Even though the clitoris is generally recognised as the hot spot for love action, the whole female pubic area can be sexually sensitive. For some women, even indirect pressure through the labia or pubic mound can lead to orgasm.

There's a horrific operation similar to male circumcision called clitoridectomy, which is carried out on women in some cultures around the world.

It involves anything from the removal of the clitoral hood, or excision; the removal of the whole clitoris, or even infibulation; the removal of all external genitalia and the stitching up of the vulva, leaving only a tiny opening for the passage of urine and menstrual blood. The operations are carried out intentionally to reduce the woman's sexual pleasure. It's illegal in the UK.

The World Health Organization claims that there are up to 90 million circumcised females alive today, mostly in Africa, the Arab States and Asia.

Stimulation

During sexual stimulation the walls of the vagina start sweating little droplets of fluid which gives it its own sensual lubrication.

The vagina itself is a tube that can expand to fit any size of penis. It can also expand to allow the head of a baby to pass through.

Insufficient lubrication before intercourse, not enough kissing, touching and clitoral contact, can cause pain during penetration, because the walls haven't lubricated themselves enough. Also, some women find it much harder to reach orgasm during penetration if they haven't been stimulated enough by hand or mouth before.

Virgin sex

There is a thin membrane called the hymen which partially blocks the entrance to the vagina.

Traditionally the hymen was supposed to be the symbol of virginity. But it's actually a very fragile thing and has usually broken away through exercise like horse riding, gymnastics or swimming, long before the first intercourse takes place.

Cervix

The cervix is the neck of the womb. It has a small opening through which menstrual blood and sperm can pass.

G spot

If men have trouble locating and dealing with the clitoris, then the G spot is going to be an even bigger problem. Most *women* couldn't tell you where their G spot was.

Named after Dr Graftenberg, the bloke who first discovered it, the G spot is a highly erotic pleasure spot located on the front wall of the vagina. But don't get in a flap if you can't find it, or even the G spot of your loved one. It's hard to find and it doesn't produce the same sensations in all women.

Most women discover it by accident during intercourse, usually when they're sitting on top of the man, or sometimes with the penis entering the vagina from behind.

GETTING TO KNOW YOUR BODY – MEN

Every man knows his penis – intimately. Spending a whole lot of time handling your hardware is all part and parcel of growing up male.

Unlike the clitoris and vagina, everything a man's got is left dangling out in the open, in what seems like a very daft bit of design.

But there is method in the madness. The main reason that a man's testicles dangle between his legs, rather than being neatly hidden in the body, is that they get too hot.

Sperm don't like to be overheated. In fact, they only work efficiently if they're stored at around 94°F/34°C, which is cooler than normal body heat. So, testicles dangle where they can be kept cool by a circulation of air.

Tight trousers and underpants or too many hot baths can decrease a man's potential for fertility because they keep the sperm too hot.

With men's wedding tackle, what you see is what you get. There aren't any hidden extras like the G spot or clitoris. And none of it's that complicated to find your way around.

Penis

The penis itself has a shaft and a head. When it's erect the head or helmet (the glans) swells and can have a purplish shiny appearance. The head of the penis is more sensitive than the shaft.

The exposed helmet is very sensitive, especially when erect and responds very kindly to soft strokings of the finger tips, but may not be at all keen on hard objects like finger nails, rings or teeth.

Slightly below the crown of the penis, on the underside, is the frenulum, a sensitive band of skin particularly well provided with nerve endings.

Penises comes in two types: with foreskin or without. Circumcision is the operation of foreskin removal. It's carried out as a matter of ritual and hygiene by some religions like the Jewish, Muslims and Coptic Christians. Many African tribes firmly believe in the practise of removing male babies' foreskins. Most Jewish boys are circumcised at eight days.

"In the hereafter Abraham will sit at the entrance of Gehinnom [Hell] and will not allow any uncircumcised Israelite to descend into it."
Talmud

Nobody really knows where the religious fashion for circumcision first came from or why. It's believed to have been practised in West Africa as much as 5000 years ago.

Some theories claim circumcision was practised for reasons of hygiene, while others claim it was a way of curbing sexual passions.

Neither theory holds any weight these days as there's no proof that circumcision affects sexual desire or sexual pleasure. Nor does having a foreskin increase your chances of catching infection or disease, so long as it's cleaned regularly.

Contrary to popular myth, there's no bone inside the penis. What makes it go erect is merely blood. Inside the penis are three long, muscular, narrow cylinders stacked with

Lots of penises bend either to the left, the right or curve upwards when they're erect. Totally straight todgers are very rare.

millions of limp balloon-like sacs. When the man gets sexually stimulated the nerve endings respond by letting loads of blood pour into the three cylinders. The valves then shut trapping the blood inside and causing the penis to stand erect.

Fact Up to eight times the normal amount of blood can be trapped inside a penis when it's erect.

Through the middle of the penis runs a tube called the urethra. This is what both urine and semen pass through on their way to the outside world.

In order to avoid peeing and ejaculating at the same time, there's a clever little valve that closes off at the neck of the bladder during ejaculation.

Beneath the penis is the scrotum which acts as a hammock for the testicles. One testicle normally hangs lower than the other. This is to avoid them being badly crushed when the man attached to them sits down quickly, cycles a racing bike or wears tight Levis. They can slot one above the other for safety.

The testicles do two main jobs, they manufacture sperm and make testosterone, the male hormone which fires up the male desire for sex and gives men their male characteristics, e.g. facial hair, deep voice, etc.

Erections

A man can get an erection for different reasons, either because he's thought about or seen something to get him aroused: a 'psychogenic' erection. Or else some form of physical touch or stimulus has made him go hard: a 'reflexogenic' erection.

Fact In 85% of men, the left testicle hangs slightly lower than the right.

Most men experience between three and five erections which might last up to half an hour each, during their sleep. Experts think that these nocturnal stiffies are only a part of the dream phase of sleep rather than actually being about any specific night-time fantasy.

Men who have serious problems with not being able to achieve erections, either through age or injury, can have surgery to help.

Vibrations can make a man's penis go erect. The vibrations of buses, coaches and lorries can have a stiffening effect on many men. This has given rise to a condition known as 'Diesel Penis' or 'Diesel Dick' where some lorry drivers have been known to suffer from frequent or even constant erections.

Fact Most men wake up with at least one erection a week.

At orgasm the sperm travel from the testes to the base of the penis where they meet up with a small walnut-sized organ called the prostate gland. It's at this gland that the semen or seminal fluid is added to the sperm.

Semen is made up of about five per cent sperm mixed in with a warm milky liquid which consists of water, proteins, simple sugars, Vitamin C, zinc and loads of other healthy stuff for the sperm to feed off as they charge off, to wherever they're heading.

Dick dimensions

One of the most common male worries men have, is that their penis isn't large enough to truly satisfy a woman during sex. Many men believe they've got a smaller than average size penis and this can cause them deep feelings of insecurity and inferiority.

"A man with a big cock is not necessarily going to be a good lover. He could have a big cock and be a lousy lover. It's not the cock that matters – it's the man."
(26 year old female)

The average length of an erect adult male penis is five and three quarter inches. Most range between five and seven inches in length, with less than ten per cent being over six and a half inches.

Fact Napoleon's penis was pickled after his death. It's now owned by an American businessman who bought it at auction for £2,600.

The penis can't be enlarged through exercise.

Most women agree that the size of the penis doesn't relate to the quality of the sex.

MASTURBATION

A brief history

> *"Be not deceived; neither fornicators...*
> *nor effeminates, nor abusers of themselves...shall inherit*
> *the kingdom of God."*
> Corinthians

Historically, masturbation has received some pretty bad Press. Ever since the Old Testament, masturbation, or 'the sin of Onan' has been seen as a distinctly dodgy pastime for men, and indeed women. In fact, the act of 'spilling your seed on the ground' could, according to the Bible, lead to eternal damnation:

What people seemed to get in a lather about most in Biblical times was that when a man was having a quick one off the wrist, he was badly wasting his valuable and sacred spunk.

> *"Every sperm is sacred*
> *Every sperm is great*
> *If a sperm is wasted*
> *God gets quite irate"*
> Monty Python,
> The Meaning of Life
> (1982)

Drives you mad

Later on though, doctors and psychiatrists decided that wanking could also directly affect the brain of the participant. Causing them to end up a good couple of sandwiches short of a picnic, so eroding the very fabric of society as a whole.

> *"Neither plague, nor war, nor smallpox, nor a crowd of similar evils have resulted more disastrously for humanity than the habit of masturbation: it is destroying the element of civilised society."*
> New Orleans Medical & Surgical Journal (1850)

Cranking cures

All those naughty boys enjoying pulling their plonkers was thought to be such a problem that the Victorians invented cruel and excruciating methods to put a stop to it. One 'cure' published in a medical journal of 1900 involved sinking two large safety pins through the perpetrator's foreskin close to the base of the penis for up to three weeks. This made erections horribly painful and masturbation totally impossible.

Everyone's at it

In recent decades, the whole guilt-trip has eased considerably and now, thankfully, wanking is looked on with a lot less shock-horror than it used to be. On the whole, experts no longer believe that it's dirty, bad or drives you mad. Which is pretty good news considering a 1970s sex report suggested that at least 98 per cent of men regularly masturbate and so do 82 per cent of women.

"Thou shalt not practise masturbation either with hand or foot."
Talmud

"Don't knock it, it's sex with someone you love."
Woody Allen in Annie Hall

"We're all wankers underneath...if we were honest about ourselves we'd know we're all wankers under the table.... I'm a wanker, I have known the pleasures of the palm. Why can't we be honest?"
Ben Elton

WHAT IS MASTURBATION?

Masturbation used to be seen as something dirty that little boys did. Eminent doctors used to claim it drove you potty and made you grow hair on the palms of your hands. Now they've mostly changed their tune and actually reckon masturbation can be *good* for you.

Masturbation is the act of giving yourself pleasure, normally by hand – but it doesn't *have* to be. And most masturbating is done by one person to themselves on their own – but again, it doesn't *have* to be.

Mutual masturbation is where lovers bring each other

to climax just through masturbating. It can also refer to the act of masturbating in front of a lover to turn them on. They might not do anything; just sit and watch. But it's still technically mutual masturbation.

BOYS MASTURBATING

Most boys learn to masturbate during their early teens. Often they learn from mates. Sometimes adolescent sexual experimentation will involve same sex mutual masturbation.

How to do it

When men jerk off they usually do it by hand, which involves holding the penis between their fingers and thumb or else clenched inside their fist. The hand is then moved up and down the length of the penis; starting with slow deliberate rythmic movements and increasing in speed as their excitment and sensation mounts.

The ultimate goal of male masturbation is ejaculation and orgasm. Some boys when they start masturbating will enjoy the sensations but not be able to ejaculate because their tackle hasn't started developing sperm yet.

Fact

A man can make himself come in less than a minute or he can make it last for hours by stopping and starting. But the average length of a male wank is between two and five minutes.

Men have been known to use objects for masturbation too. Melons and other soft fruits can be penetrated as in a sex act. And in one famous book of the 60s, *Portnoy's Complaint*, the young hero confesses to masturbating with a pound of liver bought from the butcher and then later eaten at the family dinner table. Even inflatable dolls are only elaborate masturbation aids.

Never give up on a good thing

Statistics show that nearly all men masturbate, yet they don't often talk about it. In fact, many men will deny masturbating. Some men like to pretend that it's something you do in your teens but give up when you start having 'real' sex. This is cobblers. Just because you're enjoying regular sex, is no reason to suppose you won't occasionally still want to masturbate.

> *"I love my girlfriend. I love having sex with her. But I also love to wank. I don't do it as much as I used to, but if she's not staying over, and I'm in the mood, I'll definitely have a quick one. Old habits die hard."*
>
> (23 year old male)

WOMEN AND MASTURBATION

Masturbation is still a bit of a taboo subject for women. Although practically every man masturbates, some women don't. Maybe they don't feel a need to and prefer to rely on sex for their stimulation, while others still seem to feel that it's not right or in some way dirty.

> *"I don't know why I've never done it. I've never wanted to. I like sex. I like sex a lot. But I don't like touching myself. It just feels strange."*
> (23 year old female)

How to do it

Most women who do masturbate use their fingers to tickle and stroke their clitoris and the area around it.

- some women like to use a lubricant to make the sensation smoother
- some prefer not to use their hands but to rub themselves against a soft pillow or blanket
- some even get stimulated by the sensations of a bathroom shower aimed at their clitoris and genitals
- some like to ignore the clitoris entirely to begin with, and knead the pubic mound, leaving the most sensitive area until the very end just before they climax.

The road to happy wanking is about experimenting and using your imagination. It should, by its very nature, be totally self indulgent and self pleasing. Masturbation is not about conforming to other poeple's ideas or practises. It's about self investigation and discovery.

MASTURBATION STIMULATION

One of the differences between men and women when it comes to masturbating, is that women tend to rely on mental fantasies when they're exciting themselves, whilst men often like visual stimulation. One survey suggests that 66 per cent of women fantasise when they masturbate.

"The things I think about have got nothing to do with the things that happen in real sex. I think about lesbian sex, doing it outdoors, doing it with loads of men. It's a way of letting my mind go free. It's just fantasies after all."
(29 year old female)

Fantasies for both men and women can be very tame – or get pretty wild. They can quite regularly include things like:

- your lover
- a film star
- several film stars
- members of the same sex
- members of your family
- friends
- work colleagues
- twins
- newsreaders
- or even politicians

Some people don't even think about sex when they have a hand job.

"I think about feelings, sensations. I never think about a man or actually having sex. I let my mind float away. The thoughts don't even have a form. It's like falling into a big, warm, colourful cloud."
(32 year old female)

VISUAL TURN-ON

The top shelf of every newsagent in the country is stuffed full of the sort of magazines that some men like to look at while they masturbate. Some men seem to be easily excited by photographs of naked female strangers. Pornographic videos can have the same effect. Although some women find sexual imagery exciting too, the majority of it is produced specifically for men.

"Having a wank to a dirty book is just a lot easier than thinking up sexy situations in your head. It's sexy to look at those girls. Chances are they're a lot tastier than the sort of girls you'd be likely to get off with anyway."
(23 year old male)

"Sometimes I do it four or five times a week. Sometimes I don't bother for ages. For no particular reason other than I just don't feel like it, or don't think about it."
(24 year old female)

MECHANICAL MASTURBATION

One survey claims that 17 per cent of women who masturbate use a vibrator.

Vibrators can vary enormously in size and shape:

- some are penis-shaped, ranging in size from 6 to 20 inches
- some look like torpedos

- some have ears
- some are circular – shaped like a single ball
- some have rotating heads – and look like weird DIY power tools
- some squirt a spunk-like substance

They come in battery-powered models, or even operate from the mains. They can vibrate at varying frequencies and some have two or even three speeds.

Some women enjoy the sensation of the vibrator held against the clitoris, outide the vagina, while others prefer the feel of it inserted inside.

A vibrator held against nipples, hips, buttocks, knees or thighs can all be exciting and sexually stimulating.

"Since I've discovered a vibrator I've just never looked back. It's like using a word processor instead of a manual typewriter."
(23 year old female)

You can buy vibrators in some pharmacists, sex shops, some lingerie shops and through thousands of mail order catalogue services.

Good vibrations

Vibrators can be a lot of fun and they can add a whole new dimension to your masturbating or even lovemaking. Often, discovering and experimenting with a vibrator is a sexy thing to do with your partner.

Whatever you do enjoy doing with a vibrator is not

something to be embarrassed or ashamed about. If they give you more pleasure, then the chances are they'll turn on your partner too.

Safe buzz

The only thing to remember is that vibrators can pass on STDs, especially if blood, spunk or vaginal secretions are transferred during sex. You can put a condom over most vibrators. It's important to wash them after sex. And never use them for vaginal penetration straight after anal penetration, in case you transfer germs.

WANKING IS GOOD FOR YOU

Sexologists say that masturbation can be sexually therapeutic. The act of investigating your sexual organs literally puts you in touch with your body. If you get to know the sensations that you like to feel, you'll be more able to guide a lover how to touch and excite you.

"If you can reach heights of pleasure by yourself, you're much more likely to find sexual relationships rewarding."
Dr Alan Riley, Editor of *Journal of Sexual Health*

Masturbation can be beneficial for men, because apart from giving them a knowledge of their own genitals, it can also help them to control the rate at which they reach the point of ejaculation. A stop-start masturbation technique is one of the most effective remedies against premature ejaculation.

Some men masturbate every day, twice a day. Some men do it once a week. Some might do it only twice a year. Everything is normal. Unless the masturbator becomes compulsively obsessed and masturbates continuously, there is no evidence that it does any harm at all.

> *"When I was a teenager I did it four, maybe five, maybe even six times a day. Now I'll often do it once, and I guess I'll occasionally do it twice. Maybe in the summer. I always masturbate more in the summer. It's something to do with me wearing shorts and girls wearing not a lot."*
>
> (27 year old male)

ORGASMS AND MASTURBATION

Some statistics claim that a quarter of women can only reach an orgasm through masturbation.

Because women's orgasms are less automatic than men's, they involve a fair amount of exploration, trial and error. Often it is only through masturbating and trying different ways of touching herself that a woman will be able to find just what is the right button to press, when and how, to make the orgasm happen.

> *"There's only one way that I can get an orgasm. It's always been the same. It's the way I do it myself. I have to be in the same position during sex for it to work properly."*
>
> (23 year old female)

Obviously, it has benefits when it comes to sex, because if she can then communicate the method that's most effective to her lover, then the whole business becomes much more enjoyable.

MASTURBATING IN THE MOVIES

Hollywood has realised the shock effect of showing women masturbating. Three major movies have all featured scenes with actresses pretending to have a little hand relief. In *Body of Evidence*, Madonna's seen having a little fiddle in front of Willem Dafoe, while Bridget Fonda's flatmate gets caught enjoying a Barclays Bank in *Single White Female*, and in *Sliver*, Sharon Stone's found happily having a hand shandy in the bath.

Myth

A doctor can tell if you've been masturbating. Just isn't true. There is no way a doctor can tell from an ordinary examination whether or not a man or a woman has been enjoying the pleasures of the palm.

sex

“ *I see my sexiness as my strength. I'm proud of my body. I'm not going to hide it. It's a symbol of my freedom of expression.* ”

Amanda de Cadanet

So much stuff and nonsense has been written and spoken about sex for centuries. The act of copulation, and what makes one person sexually attractive to another, has always been a source of great fascination. Incredible myths and legends had grown up around sex. Most are total tripe but they do show the depth of influence which sex has played on our imagination. As a species, we're fascinated, compelled, confused, scared and in awe of sex. Take a look at these ideas...

- In the 7th century, the Chinese believed that if a man could have sex with 93 women and stop himself from coming, it might make him a little tender but would actually give him the gift of everlasting life.

- The Swiss are supposed to believe that a man with rapidly blinking eyes has a violently passionate appetite for sex.

- Eating rotten fish and garlic is supposed to cure impotence amongst Vietnamese men.

- In parts of Africa, women achieve true sexual excitement in their men by licking his armpits.

- Men the world over think about sex every eight minutes and dream of sex three times more often than women.

- In some Eastern religions, sperm is so sacred that men are advised to ejaculate only once every ten times they have sex.

Fact Nipples didn't appear in British newspapers until the late 1960s

Does any of it make any sense?

The thing is, for most of us, sex is no longer about procreation. Most of the time we're desperate to *avoid* pregnancy. We have sex because we want to feel good and we've come to accept it as an intimate form of physical and social contact between two people.

Sex is such a powerful force in our lives but it's wrapped in so much mystery and taboo that it continually keeps us guessing unnecessarily.

In some ways, HIV and AIDS present such a horrific consequence to ignorance, that some barriers and resistance to being upfront and honest about sex, are coming down.

SAFER SEX

What is it and why should anyone want to do it?

A lot of people think that if the sex you're having is 'safer sex' then it must be boring. This is rubbish. In fact, it's quite the opposite. Instead of just having sex which is about penetration and nothing else, safer sex can be a much more involved and sensual experience.

The reason why people practise safer sex is to stop the passing on of STDs, including HIV, which is the virus which can lead to AIDS. So the reason for safer sex is sound. It's about not letting thousands of people suffer the misery of AIDS. But safer sex doesn't have to be a serious, tight-lipped affair. Far from it. Safer sex is about dim lights, soft music, warm hands, wet tongues, gentle caresses, long, deep kisses, erect nipples, stiff cocks, and soul-tugging orgasms that make your toes curl tighter than before.

Unsafe sex is where you mix body fluids with another person. Safer sex is where you don't mix body fluids. So at its most basic, safer sex could be about wearing a condom.

Safer sex is also about:

- French kissing ● buttock stroking ● masturbating
- toe sucking ● talking dirty ● strip teasing
- thigh caressing ● body rubbing ● finger fucking
- touching up ● nuzzling ● dancing naked
- fantasising ● role playing

Penetration is just one aspect of sex

With a condom, it's safer. Without a condom it's unsafe. The boring truth is that most penetration doesn't last very long. Men tend to find that just a few minutes of penetration gives enough stimulation to make them come. And afterwards, their interest in sex goes rapidly downhill.

So one way of looking at it that penetration is the start of the end in a sex session. From the moment you start penetrating, it's usually not long till you're back to the cuddling stage.

What safer sex is about is investigating and experimenting with all the other things you can do as well as penetration. Things which don't carry the same risks but do offer as much, if not more, sensual pleasure.

A lot of sex books used to talk about 'foreplay'. This was seen as a sort of sexual 'first course', where you touched, kissed and cuddled to get each other excited in order to get to the 'main course' – penetration. But gulping it down quickly to get at the meat and two veg is a mistake. It can be savoured and enjoyed for hours, and can even be enough on its own without having to move on to penetration.

> *"If anyone touches my ears,*
> *kisses them or slides their tongue inside, it sends*
> *goose pimples down my spine."*
> (23 year old female)

Most women find it easier to come with clitoral stimulation, either being caressed or masturbated by their lover's hand, or with their own hand as their lover watches. And most men can easily come by hand, by mouth, by rubbing their penis between breasts, buttocks or thighs. Penetration isn't essential. And neither is coming.

> *"If you've never licked chocolate mousse*
> *off your girlfriend's nipples, you don't know what*
> *'sexy' means."*
> (21 year old male)

Getting too caught up on achieving the goal of an orgasm can defeat the pleasure of all the other things you can do. Orgasms are great stuff but sex can be great without them too.

There's an awful lot more fun to be had without doing the obvious. The best lovers are inventive, experimental and considerate. A big, hard dick does not a good lover make.

VAGINAL SEX

The fact is, vaginal sex – where the penis enters the vagina – exists so that we can procreate. Whatever you call it: fucking, shagging, screwing, bonking, humping, playing hide the salami or doing parallel parking - it's the way that we as a species were designed to multiply. Although these days, most of the sex between men and women is done purely for pleasure.

"I love being stroked, sucked and licked, the massage and the candlelight - but there's something about feeling a man deep inside me, which takes an awful lot of beating."
(28 year old female)

A thousand and one sex guides and lover's instruction manuals will you suggest you do it upside down, back to front, sideways, in chairs, on the kitchen table and stretched out on the Axminster in front of the gas fire.

Vaginal sex is the most popular practise between

heterosexual couples. Most men can get an erection and be ready for sex quite quickly. But women need to be aroused and comfortable so that the vagina is relaxed and lubricated enough to allow the penis to enter. Whilst some women get sexual stimulation from the clitoris, others achieve orgasm through vaginal penetration. However, neither partner has to have an orgasm for it to be good sex. If the person you're doing it with is right and the feelings are good, chances are it'll warm more than your cockles.

Of course there are dangers – pregnancy and STDs (including HIV) which you can pick up from penetrating or being penetrated during vaginal sex. But if you minimise the risk by using a condom, you maximise the potential pleasure.

ORAL SEX

"You know the worst thing about oral sex? The view."
Maureen Lipman.

Lovers enjoy oral sex because it's a way of expressing deep attraction and longing. It's a way of giving each other pleasure and taking the intimacy of your sex to another more exotic, more daring level.

Oral sex means literally, 'sex of the mouth'. It comes in two basic forms; oral sex on a man or oral sex on a woman. And practically speaking, the view while you're doing either is pretty much the same.

Blow jobs

The Latin name for oral sex on a man is fellatio,
but it's most commonly called a 'blow job'.
What happens is that the penis is licked and sucked,
stroked and nibbled. All of which can feel deliciously
sensual for the owner of the penis. The sucking
might be continued to the point of orgasm and
ejaculation, or else it might just be a *part* of the
sexual fun and is followed by something else like
penetrative sex or masturbation.

Going down

Oral sex on a woman, or 'going down', is properly
known as cunnilingus. This means oral stimulation
of the vagina and clitoris by mouth, lips and tongue.
Like the penis, the clitoris responds well to warm
wet contact with a lover's mouth, and many woman
find it an exciting way to reach orgasm or just get
sexually stimulated.

Oral sex can be all or just a part of a lovemaking
episode.

Some people like to feel the sensations of their lover's
tongue and lips around their anus. This is a third form
of oral sex which is known as anilingus or 'rimming'.

Fun with fewer risks

Apart from being something lovers can enjoy
immensely, oral sex has the added advantage that it
can't get you pregnant, because sperm doesn't enter

the vagina. But sadly, that doesn't mean you won't catch sexually transmitted diseases from oral sex.

Most of the things you can catch from unprotected penetrative sex can also be caught from oral sex. HIV can be passed in menstrual blood, through bleeding gums or small cuts in either the mouth or on the genitals.

Blow jobs with the receiver wearing a condom reduces the risk of passing infections. And the advent of flavoured condoms means it can now be a total sex and taste experience.

For **cunniligus** or fanny licking, dental dams can be used to cover the vagina and clitoris. These are thin squares of latex rubber, like opened-out condoms, which are used by dentists during oral operations. If you can't get hold of a dental dam but you want to practise safer cunnilingus, you can cut down the side of a condom and open it out to cover the bit you want to lick and suck.

Anilingus carries a greater risk potential in terms of catching infections, mainly because there are more germs on offer around this part of the body. So use a dental dam.

Fact 'Soixante neuf' or '69er' are the slang names gives to practising mutual oral sex, because like the figure 69, while licking and sucking each other, a couple can lie head to toe.

GIVING'S AS GOOD AS GETTING

Oral sex is a very intense sort of sex. You literally
have your face buried in the most erogenous zone of
your lover. All you can see smell and taste is sex.
It can be a heady and intoxicating sensation.

It's not everyone's cup of tea

Some people don't like their sex to get that intimate
or that messy. But for some people the intensity and
even the flavours of giving oral sex can be immensely
exciting.

Pleasure in giving

There's also the feeling of giving pleasure. Although
there is a hugely enjoyable physical side of giving oral
sex, there is also the other aspect of it which is about
knowing you're making your lover happy. Giving
pleasure to someone brings its own rewards.

Sexy smells

Many people are scared that their lover will be put
off by their genital smell. This is one of the fears
that puts a lot of people off letting their lover lick and
suck them. But often it is exactly this smell of sex
which is so succulent and enjoyable. For this same
reason, it's not a good idea to swamp your tackle in
deodorants or body sprays. Of course it's good to be
clean and recently bathed, but giving your lover a

mouthful of deodorant is likely to be much more off-putting than your natural sexy smell.

ANAL SEX

Unlike the vagina, the anus wasn't really designed to have a penis thrust into it. But then again, nor was the mouth, yet oral sex feels very good to the receiver and often to the giver too.

The same goes for anal sex. The anus is a tight ring of muscle which can exert a lot of pleasant pressure on the penis. Some men like anal sex because they prefer the sensation of the anal ring against their penis. Some gay men practise anal sex as a pleasurable alternative to oral or non-penetrative sex.

Not all gay men practise anal sex by any means. In fact, the numbers who do have fallen steeply since the discovery of HIV. At the same time there are many straight couples who enjoy anal sex.

"Most girls aren't interested in letting you inside their anus. A few are though, the more experimental ones. It feels good. Although sometimes it's hard to come. I like doing it but that doesn't mean I'm gay."
(27 year old male)

Surprisingly, the law states that anal sex or 'sodomy' is only allowed between males over the age of consent. But it's not recognised as legal for a man to have anal sex with a woman, at any age, even if they're married.

Some men and some women enjoy having a penis inside their anus because they find the physical sensations exciting and revel in the feeling of being able to give to their lover.

> *"There's nothing else like it.
> When it's good, it's heaven."*
> (22 year old male)

Not safer sex

Anal sex is probably the least safe form of sex you can have. It's potentially bad news because it's easy to transmit sexually transmitted diseases including things like rectal gonorrhoea, hepatitis B and HIV.

The dangers are increased because the rectum is very delicate and its tissues tear easily when penetrated. Its tightness also means that the penetrating penis will suffer lots of tiny surface tears too. So, there's an easy passage of blood between the two lovers, which immediately raises the risk of transmitting infections, including HIV.

The greatest risk is to the person being penetrated although it's still very risky for the man penetrating during anal intercourse.

Making it safer

The safest way to approach anal sex is:

● **For the penetrator to wear a condom heavily lubricated with a water-based lubricant like KY jelly. This reduces**

the friction, so there's less damage to the surface of the
penis and rectal passage, as well as less strain on the
condom which may otherwise split.
- Use condoms which are thicker than standard ones, like
  Durex Extra Strong or Superstrong Mates. These are much
  less likely to tear or split during anal sex.
- It may help to use a condom lubricated with nonoxynol-9,
  a lubricating substance which is also a spermicide and able
  to kill a wide range of bacteria. The ingredient that kills
  sperm can also kill some STD bacteria and viruses. The only
  problem is that although these are proven safe for vaginal
  intercourse, they may not be safe to use in the rectum.
- Use lots of lubricant on the anus before penetration.
- Penetrate slowly and gently, maybe even with the receiver
  on top, so that they can control the amount and the pace of
  penetration.
- Although on paper, it's illegal for heterosexual couples to
  have anal sex, a lot of couples do it – and enjoy it. One risk
  that heterosexual couples must beware of, is not
  penetrating the vagina straight after penetrating the anus,
  without washing the penis. Bacteria can easily be passed
  from the anus to the vagina and can cause vaginal
  infections.

*"I've done it a couple
of times. And I can't say I got a lot out
of it. The first time it really hurt and I had to stop
him. It did get easier after that but not what you'd call sexy.
I've known a few boyfriends who've wanted to try it.
Blokes seem intrigued by it."*
(26 year old female)

Chapter 4

Talking about sex

> 66 Having a damn good talk with a guy is just as exciting as sex. 99

Jodie Foster

Not everyone is going to agree with Jodie Foster that talk is an excellent substitute for sex. But what most people will agree on is that talking about sex is an immensely tricky business.

Bike shed banter

Firstly, there's the sort of talking about sex that you do with your friends when you're going through puberty. Usually this has a good naughty buzz, but what gets learnt is basically a mishmash of misinformed nonsense.

> *"We talked about sex loads of times when we were having a fag behind the bikesheds. Talked about it for years and years - but I swear to God none of us had a clue what it was really like."*
> (26 year old male)

Parental guidance

> *"My mum told me everything I needed to know."*
> Mandy Smith

Then there's the talking that your parents *might* do with you in your early adolescence, telling you about sex, periods and the making of babies.

"My old man once said
to me 'D'you know the about the birds
and the bees?' I said 'Yeah'. And he said 'Good'.
End of conversation. I never discussed anything
like that with my mum either."
Tom Jones

An awful lot of people admit that their parents never
told them anything about sex or anything that was
any use. And even amongst those who did have talks,
some either felt enormously embarrassed or else
badly disappointed.

"I was 12 when my
dad decided we should have this 'little talk'.
He started off asking me if I knew the difference
between me and my sister. I said 'Yeah. She's called Laura and
couldn't play football if her life depended on it'. I just couldn't
face him talking about sex. So I just kept cracking jokes."
(22 year old male)

"My aunty told me
about sex and boys. She said there were things
I should know. But what she actually told me was
so pathetic and childish, I almost started to tell her
things. It was obvious that even at 12, I knew
a lot more than she did."
(20 year old female)

Sex at school

And of course there's sex education at school. Some people's experience of formal sex education isn't very encouraging.

"In biology all we learnt about was rabbits and viruses. Nothing was ever said about humans."
(21 year old female)

Sadly, even in a period of time in which the threat of HIV and AIDS makes ignorance about sexual matters potentially fatal, there's still a big problem with talking about sex in schools.

In July 1993, the Government passed the Sex Education Amendment No 62 to the Education Bill. Secondary schools will still have to provide sex education, including information on AIDS, HIV, STDs and aspects of human sexual behaviour. But references to these topics, other than biological aspects, have been removed from the National Curriculum. And parents can withdraw their children from sex education lessons outside of the National Curriculum.

When talking is taboo

The problem is that if you're brought up to think that it's not nice to talk about sex, then the chances are you'll *never* be comfortable talking about it. But it's difficult to learn anything sensible about sex and sexuality, or being able to gets your sexual needs met or being able to express yourself freely, in a sexual way, if you don't *talk* about sex.

Lovers and friends

The most relevant people to talk about sex with in adult life are your lovers; to tell them what you need, want and feel. And your friends. Because sex is such a taboo subject, a lot of people start to think that they're weird or abnormal if they have sexual problems. But checking it out with your peers often proves that everyone else has experienced something very similar.

In a recent survey, 75 per cent of people said they felt uncomfortable expressing their innermost sexual desires and fantasies to their partner. The truth is, talking about sex can not only improve the quality of your relationship, it can also add an extra dimension to your lovemaking.

"Sometimes I just tell him all the things I want to do to him or I want him to do to me. I just let my mouth and my imagination run a bit wild. It sounds daft but it's dead exciting to do."
(25 year old female)

TIPS ON TALKING ABOUT SEX

● *If you want to change something that happens – or doesn't happen – with a regular partner*, be diplomatic. Don't accuse. Try saying it positively, say "I'd really love it if you...." rather than "Why do you never...."*

- *If there's something you want to happen – talk about it before you get too far down the line and then feel disappointed.* Bring talk into your sex. Say when something feels good. Ask for what you want. Make noises of appreciation.
- *Look into each other's eyes.* Too many lovers never look at each other when they have sex. Communication is more than words.
- *Talking about sex when you're not in bed can be an effective way of getting you both excited.* It's also a time when you can think about what you want to say with a clear head.
- *Never be afraid to say no to something you don't really like.*
- *Don't be shy to ask for what you want or dream about –* you never know, you might be voicing your partner's own secret desire. Whatever it is, there's certainly no harm in asking.

TALK DIRTY AMONGST YOURSELVES

An awful lot of people find it difficult to talk about sex, but it's generally agreed, especially by men, that women talk more about sex than men do. Research shows that men between the ages of 18 and 24 are likely to believe their girlfriends talk far too much about sex.

Women tend to talk about sex in a different way to men

A lot of the time, men don't talk about sex with each other at all. If they do, often it's not about the act itself, certainly it's rarely about the emotions involved. Men often feel the need to get all macho and confine their conversation to the girlfriend's physical attributes; the size of her breasts or the sexual things she did. They'll talk about where and how many times they did it. But almost never would they admit to failure, problems or sexual dissatisfaction.

> *"It's one thing telling your mates who you've shagged and who you'd like to shag. It's another thing telling them you often get premature ejaculation or can't get a hard on!"*
> (25 year old male)

Women go into detail

Women don't seem to be so worried about being judged by their peers as men. And they're more used to revealing themselves and even appearing vulnerable in conversation. A small group of girls might divulge private details about themselves and so encourage each other to do the same. It works almost like a form of group therapy with an exchange of information and education. This just doesn't happen amongst heterosexual men.

Women are more honest

Women tend to be more happy to own up to past difficulties and share honest experiences, because they don't feel so threatened by their peers. They don't feel they have something to prove in the same way that some men do.

Sex talk is good for you

Talking about sex that was bad, unsatisfying or upsetting can be a very good way of dealing with the unpleasant feelings. Sharing the experience of an unhappy sexual episode can give you some power over the past. Telling friends allows you to hear their views too. Maybe it's happened to them hundreds of times. Who knows, maybe talking will even help you to see the funny side of it all.

TALKING DIRTY TO EACH OTHER

Being able to talk about sex with the person you're having sex with sounds as though it should be easy. But for very many lovers it isn't.

A recent survey showed a low proportion of both sexes claim to not be satisfied with the level of communication that goes on in the bedroom only 34 per cent of men and 28 per cent of women felt they were talking enough about sex with their partners.

Most people felt they didn't talk about sex enough, but reckoned *they* weren't to blame:

- One in six said that they felt their partners didn't talk enough about sex.
- A small percentage of people claimed they couldn't talk about sex with their partner because they wouldn't take them seriously.

Although it's now universally agreed that talking about sex; explaining your needs, moods and preferences

with your lover is a useful way of achieving better sex
and a better relationship, it still doesn't make it easy.

Language

The language of sex is a problem. So many of the
sex words are also swear words and insults that they
become uncomfortable to use in a loving situation.

One way round this is to develop your own language
that you and your lover use exclusively together. It
might be easier to handle and give you a few added
laughs into the bargain.

Need trust to talk

Talking about your innermost feelings and desires
makes you feel vulnerable. If you talk about your
sex, you expose a part of you that normally remains
hidden. And so to be able to expose this part
of you, it's important to feel absolutely safe
and to totally trust your lover.

*"I could talk to my
girlfriend about everything. Well, everything except some
things to do with sex."*
(29 year old male)

TALKING ABOUT SEX BEFORE IT HAPPENS

Talking about sex with a prospective lover before
you've had sex can be immensely difficult. The main
problem is that we want it to happen without being

discussed, just in case we're wrong about their feelings towards us.

> "Sitting on this wall she just said 'Do you want to have rampant sex with me tonight?'. She was joking in a sense of being serious. I say those sort of things too. You have to exaggerate and joke because you can't say 'Okay seriously, do you want to make love with me tonight?'. If you make a joke out of it, then it's alright, it puts the point across but it's still subtle."
> (19 year old male)

Too much – too soon

Embarrassment plays a big part in it all. The fear is that if you appear too pushy, or confident or over keen, then the other person will recoil and reject you. By being too upfront, you worry that you could scupper your chances.

Scared of speaking out

The other big issue when it comes to discussing the sex that *might* be about to happen, is indecision. If you're undecided as to what you should or shouldn't do, there's a temptation to leave it up to the other person and the mood of the situation to make up your mind for you. By stopping the proceedings and saying something like "Are we going to make love?", then you're crystallising the dilemma: Whether to have sex or not. A lot of people simply don't want to make the decision, because *they're* not sure what they want to happen.

No talk – no control

The problem with not crystallising the situation into words is that you then lose control of what's about to happen. And entering into a sexual encounter with someone who you've not discussed sex with, means that you run the risk of maybe having unsafe sex without a condom, or being urged or forced into doing something sexual that you really don't want to do.

> *"It sounds corny, but what I do if things are going real fast, is say 'Woa, this really intense – can we just take a breather?' It gives me a chance to get my bearings. Usually means you talk a bit too."*
> (20 year old male)

Letting things go too far

Too many people find themselves in situations where they are too embarrassed to say no, or to insist on safer sex, because they feel responsible for letting the circumstances unfold so far without having said something earlier.

> *"All my friends had
> slept with someone and I hadn't.
> So it was the expected thing to do. I didn't want to but
> I felt it'd look stupid if I said no, because I knew
> all my friends had."*
> (18 year old female)

Taking control

Taking control of the situation before it becomes a sort of sexual snowball with a momentum of its own, is the most effective thing to do. It avoids hurting anyone's feelings, avoids misunderstandings and most of all means that you don't have to do something you'll regret.

Losing the moment

People complain that talking about sex before it happens takes the romance and spontaneity out of sex. Trouble is, spontaneity all too often leads to pregnancy, regret and STDs.

Straight talk can be sexy

Talking about sex before it happens, doesn't have to be scary or boring, it can be immensely sexy.

If you want to talk about sex before it happens:

- be direct
- make yourself clear
- don't be timid
- don't use medical sounding words

- don't feel embarrassed
- say: "I don't want to just do it. I want to talk about it first."
  - or "I can't relax if I feel I'm in bed with a silent stranger."
  - or "Talk to me – that's what gets me hot."
  - or "The sexiest things you can do with your lips is *talk* to me."

"It worked a charm. All I did was hold his cock in the palm of my hand, it was stiff as a board and I could feel it throbbing. I looked him in the eyes and said 'You know there's only two things that I want in the world right now – your cock deep inside me ... and your cock inside a condom'. I've never seen anyone get one on so fast!"

(27 year old female)

TALKING ABOUT SEX WHILE YOU'RE DOING IT

There are two types of talking you can do while you're having sex; there's the recreational and the educational.

The recreational is where you talk dirty, give encouragement, or simply shout, grunt and whoop with delight.

The educational is where you talk to explain how you like to be touched, or ask what your partner would like you to do for them. It's where you guide each other to do things that make your sex more exciting, happy and varied.

How to talk dirty

Talking dirty in your lover's ear, or else having smutty things whispered in your own pink shell-like during sex, can be a corker. Many lovers definitely get off on it.

"I say awful things to him. I can't believe some of the stuff I come out with. Really dirty. Things I want him to do to me. Things I'm going to do to him.... I love it. And he certainly never complains."
(30 year old female)

As with so many things about sex, the fact that some people like it a lot, doesn't mean that everyone does, and some won't like it at all. So it's important that you approach the whole business gently. Try it out, see if you get a favourable reaction.

Maybe even check it out afterwards, ask your partner what they thought when you said what you did during sex. If they say they were turned on by it, then you know you're on to a winner. If they turn pale and say 'I've never heard anything so depraved and despicable in my whole life' then chances are you'd best leave that technique alone.

Gently at first

Talking dirty can be done in a mild and encouraging way by simply telling your lover how much you love their body, their kisses, their breasts, chest, muscles, back – whatever lights your fire. This works well because it's encouraging and flattering, but it also establishes an intimate verbal communication during sex, which otherwise can get a bit isolated if each partner is just stuck in their own sensual world.

Digging deeper

Talking dirty can go deeper, where you both start saying things to each other which would seem totally inappropriate in any other context. Often it involves using words like 'cunt', 'fuck', 'cock' or talking about 'hot cum', 'love seeds', 'joy juice' or whatever trips off the tongue. It's using the dirty language of sex to make the act seem more naughty and exciting. It's about revelling in the repression of sex and its taboos.

Some people find talking dirty very liberating and satisfying. It's not just about the sex, it's also about learning to really let yourself go. Part of the reason why many people find sex difficult is that they don't find it easy to get out of themselves. Talking dirty might well help you get out of the intellectual person and totally into the physical. A change, as they say, is as good as a rest.

Natural sighs

A lot of the most natural communication that takes place during sex is non-verbal. It's body language; a gesture here or a hug there. Or else it's by sounds rather than words. Moans, whimpers, sighs and squeals.

All those sounds of sex can mean an awful lot to

your partner. If your lover gives a horny moan as you touch them or a satisfying sigh as they come, those sounds alone can speak a thousand words in terms of your *own* pleasure. You can really get off on knowing that your lover is having a good time.

Making changes

Sometimes sighs aren't enough, particularly if there's some pattern of behaviour you want to change or something new you want to try.

The best way to talk about things you don't want or things you want to change is to be positive and not to criticise. Sex can be such a sensitive spot in people's image of themselves that it's important to always tread lightly.

If you're not sure if something you're doing is being well received, then it's always good to ask. When it comes to caressing a clitoris or playing with a penis, asking for directions works:

- **"Does that feel nice?"**
- **"Am I touching you right?"**
- **"Tell me what it feels like"**
- **"Do you want it harder or softer?"**

Show and tell

What can be even more exciting is to actually take your partner's hand and lower it to the area in question saying 'Why don't you *show* me just how you like it'. Feeling your partner feeling themselves in a sexual way can be an enormously erotic sensation.

Other people's bodies are a mystery. We know what feels good for ourselves but what things feel like to others is impossible to know.

The best way to find out is to show and tell.

Orgasm talk

Talking through an orgasm is something that some people love to do. Others don't want to utter a word or a sound, they want to be left totally alone to get on with their personal pleasure.

The big benefit of talking about your orgasm; to say when you think you're about to come; to say how it *feels*; to vocalise the sensations, is that you share the pleasure with your partner.

To hear your lover getting more and more excited, and for them to say exactly when they're about to come or are actually coming, can be humungously enjoyable.

> *A recent survey claimed that 14% said their partners weren't emotional enough when it came to sex.*

It's like being let in on a beautifully sexy secret.

Fact

In the Solomon Islands, instead of saying anything, women bite their partners on orgasm. The more teeth marks a man displays, the better the lover he's meant to be.

AFTER SEX

Sexual post mortems can be horrible. All that "how was it for you?" stuff can be cringingly hammy. A lot of the time that sort of "did you come?" talk is just about making the asker feel better about their performance.

Talking about what you've done after you've done it can work wonders though. To say, "God I really loved it when you did that …" and then to be specific, can set you up marvellously for next time. If you take care to point out the stuff that really watered your garden, then at least your partner knows for future reference.

And in a way, talking about it afterwards can prolong the intimacy and make a gentle rehabilitation back into the non-sexual world. It can be a bit weird if you've been having an intimate sexual experience, then after it's over one of you jumps up to put the kettle on and neither of you really knows what to say or do. But to lie together a little longer and mull over a couple of the sexy moments you shared brings the sex to a gentler conclusion.

ALL TALK NO SEX

Mind and body warm up

A bit of dirty talk can be a marvellous way of warming up your mind and body *before* having sex. The titillating powers of a few whispered sexy words, either just before you have sex, or even on the bus home, after a date, ages before you get round to going to bed, can be a lovely aperitif to sex.

But talking about sex doesn't have to be part of actually having sex; it can be *instead* of having sex.

Telephone sex

Even talking on the phone to your lover and straying onto sexy subjects can be an enormously exciting experience. It could be heightened by touching yourself intimately as you talk and listen. You might not even need to touch yourself, the words themselves might make your cockles glow sufficiently bright.

"The first time we did it was in this posh restaurant after dinner. I said that she looked really sexy and I wanted to take her home and make love. Then she said she wanted to suck me. And I said I wanted to cup her breasts and lick her nipples. And it went on like that. We looked like we were just having a normal chat."
(26 year old male)

Not always easy to say no

Saying no isn't always easy. We should all know that we have the absolute right to say no and stop any sexual proceedings at whatever stage, whenever we want to. None of us should feel obliged or forced to do anything sexual against our will. But it's not always as straightforward as that.

71

A lot of the time people don't say no to sex because they feel guilty. There's often a sense that because you've given the other person encouragement up to a point, then it's your duty to follow through. But what this means is that you ultimately end up having sex which you'd really rather not be having.

It happens easily. You might meet someone and be instantly attracted to them and think you want to sleep with them. But then, several hours later when push comes to shove, you actually decide you don't like them that much and *don't* want to have sex with them. You need to be able to say no. Otherwise you sell yourself short and end up hating yourself, the sex and them.

No one has rights over your body

"It was a mistake to start having sex with him. I wanted to at first, but then I went off sex – and him. Every time he's come round he'd keep demanding it. He'd say 'we've done it before and you liked it so why can't we do it now?' I never really had a good answer."
(24 year old female)

Just because you've had sex with someone in the past, doesn't give them any rights over you. Every time you have sex, your feelings should be suitable. You should want to do it and look forward to the sensations, not feel dread or obligation. If you do, it's a safe bet the sex will not make you feel good or happy.

It can be hard to say no to a regular partner because you're frightened of hurting them. So you may have sex that you don't really want. The risk with this is that a resentment builds up through being dishonest about your true feelings which does eventually affect your feelings about sex and your partner.

"He'd do it three times a night if I'd let him. I'm just not that interested. It's not that I don't love him or don't enjoy sex, I just don't need it that often."
(27 year old female)

In a long-term relationship it's always better to talk things through tenderly and thoughtfully. Rather than just saying "No way José", to explain that you don't really feel like it and would rather just have a cuddle makes it easier to handle.

Rejection's never that easy to take, but if it's done with kindess it's a whole lot nicer. It's important to avoid ever turning sex into something angry or contentious. Being mean with each other over sex can spoil it.

Don't be vague

Saying no in a sexual situation with someone you don't know very well, has to be done clearly. Be assertive and use your body language to emphasise what you're saying. The earlier you do it, the better. And if you're in doubt, don't hestitate. Don't wait and think you'll make your mind up later, do it before things go too far.

Don't take risks

Although we should all be able to stop anything sexual from being forced upon us or done out of obligation, it's best not to test this right. Don't get into sexual situations that you feel unsure about with people you don't trust. Just because you *should* be able to stop it doesn't mean you always will.

Chapter 5

Contraception

" Contraceptives
should be used on
all conceivable
occasions. "

**Spike
Milligan**

THE HOW-TO OF CONTRACEPTION

Sex may be fun, but it needs some serious thought too. If you want to avoid sexually transmitted diseases (see page 125) and pregnancy (see page 107), you have to get yourself kitted out with some form of adequate contraception. Male or female, it's your responsibility.

What is contraception?

Contraception is the taking of measures to prevent conception and pregnancy. In days of old, some weird methods were used, like putting a half lemon over the cervix, making plugs out of lint and honey or even inserting a sponge soaked in vinegar. But none of the ancient contraceptive ideas got much weirder than this:

"If a woman hangs about her neck the finger and anus of a dead foetus, she will not conceive ... If one takes the two testicles of a weasel and wraps them up, binding them to the thigh of a woman who wears also a weasel bone on her person, she will no longer conceive."
The Admirable Secrets of Albert the Great (16th century)

These days there are more reliable methods around. And certain methods like the condom, can also help prevent STDS. Here's a guide to what's on offer ...

Condoms

For many years, condoms were only worn by men, but the female condom has been available since 1992. Both work by preventing the man's sperm from coming into contact with the woman's vagina. Sperm is caught in the condom, so there's little chance of it meeting and fertilising the egg. The **male condom** is a soft, stretchy tube, usually made of latex rubber and designed to fit snugly over the penis. The **female condom** is a slightly wider tube, made of polyurethane plastic. Its brand name is Femidom. It's shaped much like the male condom but has a flexible rubber ring at each end. For more on both condoms see page 89.

Advantages: Easy to get hold of. Easy to use. Don't need medical advice to fit them. Can protect against cervical cancer. Protects both partners against some STDs, including HIV.

Disadvantages: Some people say they interfere with the 'flow' of sex as you have to stop and put one on – but some people make that part of sex. Some people react to the rubber/spermicide used to coat them. Male condoms aren't suitable for men who regularly lose their erection during sex. Female condoms are no good for women who have vaginal or cervical infections or who don't like touching their genitals.

Myth You can't get pregnant if you do it standing up. Yes you can.

Reliability: If used according to the instructions, the male condom is 98% reliable (i.e. about two women in every 100 couples who use condoms properly get pregnant).

SPERMICIDES Many male condoms are lubricated with a substance that kills sperm, but some are not, so you may have to use spermicide. The female condom is lubricated but not with spermicide.

Using extra spermicide with a condom is a good way to be sure of avoiding pregnancy.

Some spermicides cause irritations. If this happens, stop using it and seek medical advice.

Contraceptive implants

Contraceptive implants are small soft tubes which are placed under the skin (usually on the inner upper arm). A tiny incision is made under local anaesthetic and six tubes are inserted. Once in place, you can feel them but you can't see them. They release progestogen into the bloodstream over five years. It works by thickening the cervical mucus making it difficult for sperm to get through. It also alters the lining of the womb, making it less likely to accept a fertilised egg. In some cases, it stops ovulation.

Myth You can't get pregnant if you do it when the man is drunk as the alcohol kills his sperm. Yes you can.

Advantages: Highly effective. Good for people who aren't too good at remembering to take pills or can't use other methods of contraception. Doesn't get in the way of sex. Can be used safely when breastfeeding. Fertility returns as soon as the implant is removed. You can have it removed as soon as you decide you no longer want it.

Disadvantages: Periods change. Minor side-effects in some women.

Reliability: Over one year, it's about 99%. Over the whole five years, it's about 98% effective.

Contraceptive injections

Contain a similar hormone to that in the progestogen-only pill. One injection gives contraceptive protection for 8 or 12 weeks, depending on type of injection.

Advantages: Only need injections every two or three months. Doesn't interfere with lovemaking.

Disadvantages: Once you've been injected, effects (and side-effects) won't wear off for another three months. On stopping injections, can take up to a year or more for periods and fertility to return to normal. Periods may change.

Reliability: Highly effective: over 99%.

Diaphragms and caps

Caps and diaphragms fit over the cervix, preventing

sperm from entering the womb. All are made of rubber and are used with a spermicide. A doctor or nurse will teach you how to use one. It has to be left in for a minimum of six hours (and up to 30 hours) after intercourse. Wash after use and store in its container in a cool, dry place.

Advantages: No side-effects for most women. May protect against cervical cancer and some STDs.

Disadvantages: Need to plan ahead. Has to be used with spermicide. Can take a while to learn how to use one. Some people react to the rubber or spermicide, and some women get cystitis. Have to be checked regularly for damage. Need to be replaced if you gain or lose weight (3 kg), after having a baby and after a miscarriage or abortion. Need a checkup every 12 months, to make sure it's still the right fit.

Reliability: Highly effective: 98%.

Intrauterine devices (IUD)

They are about 4 cms long, made of plastic and copper wire and fit inside the womb. At the bottom end is a thread, which hangs out through the cervix and into the vagina.

Myth You can't get pregnant if you have sex when you're having a period. Yes you can.

Advantages: Doesn't interrupt intercourse. Works as soon as it's been inserted.

Disadvantages: Not suitable for women who are not in mutually faithful sexual relationships. Some women get pelvic infections. Can cause heavier or longer periods or breakthrough bleeding in some women. So they're not recommended for women who already have heavy periods. Occasionally, the IUD can come out.

Reliability: Over 98% effective.

Natural methods

The idea is generally not to have sex at the woman's most fertile time. The most reliable is called the 'sympto-thermal method' which relies on temperature-keeping and noticing the changes in the vaginal fluids.

Advantages: No mechanical devices or hormones used. No side-effects. Good for people who choose not to use other methods of contraception.

Disadvantages: Need to be taught by trained teacher. Need to keep careful records every day. Needs a co-operative partner. Have to obtain and use another method of contracption if you want to have sex during the woman's fertile time.

Reliability: Used in a careful and committed way about 98% effective. With less care, it can drop to 80% or less.

COITUS INTERRUPTUS (WITHDRAWAL) This is such an unreliable method of contraception that it shouldn't really be classed as contraception at all! It's where the male withdraws his penis from the woman's vagina before ejaculation.

Advantages: No prior planning or supplies needed.

Disadvantages: Loads – from unsatisfying sex to pregnancy to infection with STDs.

Reliability: Not good. Most men produce some semen during sex prior to ejaculation and this alone can cause pregnancy. Even if you could be sure that he doesn't produce a drop, chances of getting pregnant are still pretty high.

Oral contraceptives ('the Pill')

COMBINED PILL Usually called 'the Pill'. Contains two hormones – oestrogen and progestogen. Works by stopping the ovaries releasing an egg each month.

Advantages: Easy and convenient to use. Doesn't get in the way of sex. Periods are shorter, lighter and less painful. PMT and other period-associated problems alleviated. Offers some protection against cancer of the womb and ovaries, fibroids, ovarian cysts, some pelvic infections and benign breast disease.

Myth You can't get pregnant if the man doesn't come inside you. Yes you can.

Disadvantages: Can cause minor side-effects in some women although these often disappear after a while. Health risks are increased for smokers over 35. Less effective if you miss a pill, if you're taking certain medicines, or if you have severe diarrhoea or vomiting. After you stop taking the Pill it *may* take some time for periods and fertility to return to normal.

Reliability: Over 99% when used properly, much lower when not.

PROGESTOGEN-ONLY PILL It has to be taken at the same time every day. It works by causing changes in the cervical mucus which make it difficult for a man's sperm to enter the womb, or accept a fertilised egg. It sometimes prevents ovulation.

Advantages: Same as for the combined pill (above). Useful for older women who smoke. You can use it when you're breastfeeding.

Disadvantages: May not work if taken more than three hours late. Vomiting, severe diarrhoea, or certain medicines can also reduce its effectiveness. Some women may have side-effects but they usually last only two or three months. Periods might not be regular. If you're over 11 stone (70 kg) it may make this Pill less effective.

Reliability: 99% with careful use, much less if not.

Myth You can't get pregnant if you're breastfeeding. Yes you can.

Sponge

It's a soft, round sponge containing spermicide which covers a woman's cervix. It works for 24 hours and has to be left in for 6 hours after intercourse. Dispose of carefully in a bin.

Advantages: Same as the cap and diaphragm (see above). You can buy them in pharmacists: one size fits all!

Disadvantages: Expensive and not at all reliable when used on its own. Can only be used once (although you can have intercourse as often as you like for 24 hours). Doesn't protect you from all STDs.

Reliability: Used properly, about 90% effective. When used less carefully, this falls to around 75%.

Surgical methods

STERILISATION FOR WOMEN The Fallopian tubes (which carry the egg to the womb) are cut or blocked. It doesn't affect periods, sex or sex drive, but prevents conception.

Advantages: Very effective for couples who know they don't want any (or any more) children. Effective immediately after the operation.

Disadvantages: Some women have heavier periods.

Myth You can't get pregnant if you don't have an orgasm. Yes you can.

Sterilisation is permanent.

Reliability: Almost 100%.

STERILISATION FOR MEN (VASECTOMY) A minor operation in which the vas deferens (sperm-carrying tubes) in a man's scrotum are snipped and tied. Semen is still produced but contains no sperm. It takes up to 16 weeks for all sperm to be drained however, so another method of contraception should be used for at least four months after the operation.

Advantages: Same as sterilisation for women (see above).

Disadvantages: It's permanent.

Reliability: Almost 100%.

Emergency contraception

If you've had sex without contraception or you think that your chosen method has failed, don't panic. There are two very effective emergency measures you can take:

THE "EMERGENCY" PILL The woman is given two special doses of the Pill. These must be prescribed by a doctor and taken 12 hours apart.

Advantages: Almost always works.

Myth You can't get pregnant the first time you have sex. Yes you can.

Disadvantages: Can make you feel sick. If you do vomit, you need to get more pills. Not for regular use.

Reliability: This method is highly effective (about 95–99%)

THE "EMERGENCY" IUD. A doctor fits an IUD and if this is done within five days of unprotected sex, pregnancy should be prevented.

Advantages: Highly effective, and once it's fitted it can be left in place and used as an on-going method of contraception.

Disadvantages: Not suitable for all women. Check with your doctor.

Reliability: Almost 100%.

WHERE TO GO FOR CONTRACEPTION

You can go to one of four places...

- Your own GP
- A different (i.e. not your usual) GP
- A family planning clinic
- A youth advisory service

Wherever you go, you'll be advised on the method that's most suitable for your lifestyle and

Myth You can't get pregnant if you have a bath straight afterwards. Yes you can.

relationship. Your GP may not be able to provide the service you require, but will be able to point you in the direction of your nearest family planning clinic. They can provide emergency contraception, pregnancy testing, help and advice with an unplanned pregnancy, abortion referral, information about all contraception including male and female sterilisation, safer sex advice, free condoms, advice on sexual problems and sexual health and cervical smear tests. Family planning clinics can also refer you to agencies which can help with infertility, sexually transmitted diseases and genetic counselling.

Where do I find a GP?

Get names and addresses of local GPs from libraries, post offices, phone books, advice centres and Family Health Services Authorities. GPs who give contraceptive advice have the letter 'C' after their name.

Where do I find a family planning clinic?

Get addresses and opening times from health centres, hospitals, the phone book, your GP, advice centres, the local district health authority or the Family Planning Association. See p 138 for address. They can

Myth You might get pregnant if you take a bath in a man's water. No you can't.

provide leaflets on contraception in Welsh, Bengali, Gujarati, Hindi, Punjabi and Urdu, and some clinics employ staff who can speak these and other languages.

What about Youth Advisory Services?

Young people are welcome to go to any GP or family planning clinic for contraception advice. In fact, some GPs and clinics run special youth sessions. Brook Advisory Centres offer a free and confidential service to all teenagers and young people. Under 16s are also welcome. They run clinics in nine cities in England. See page 139.

> *"I want to tell you a terrific story about oral contraception ... she said 'No'."*
> Woody Allen

Remember, even if you're using other forms of contraception, a condom is the best way to protect yourself from sexually transmitted diseases, including HIV.

Myth You might get pregnant from oral sex. No you can't.

Chapter 6

Condoms

66 *Condoms are such a drag. . .*
they interrupt
everything. . . they're not great
but they make sense.
They've saved my life. 99

Madonna

BRITISH STANDARD BS 3704 CERTIFIED TO

From Egypt to Nuneaton: a short history of the condom

1350 BC The condom started off life not to prevent pregnancy, but as a way of stopping the transmission of diseases. It's reported that Egyptian tribesmen used them as protection against infection, injury and insect bites.

16th c. An Italian anatomist called Gabrielle Fallopius claimed to have invented condoms made of linen to guard against syphilis.

18th c. Condom shops were flourishing by now. Condoms were still essentially seen as barriers against disease. Although some people had twigged they had contraceptive qualities too.

19th c. The Japanese were using condoms made out of leather.

1921 The first clinic set up to distribute condoms had been founded in Britain by Marie Stopes.

1932 Durex set up a manufacturing plant in Hackney, east London, and started churning out condoms big time.

1934 The first female condom manufactured.

1953 The first electronic testing machine developed.

1957 The first lubricated condom slipped onto the streets.

1968 The first deal to supply condoms through pubs.

1980 Asda became the first supermarket to stock condoms.

1987 TV advertisements for condoms were allowed for the first time.

1992 The very first free-standing street vending machine for condoms was installed at Nuneaton bus station.

TRIED AND TESTED

In Britain, certain condoms carry the **British Standards Institution Kitemark**. This means they have been through rigorous tests for strength and reliability. These are the safest condoms to use.

Other countries have their own safety tests but at the moment there's no recognised internationally agreed standard so it's difficult to know which imported brands are safe.

Every packet of condoms should have an **expiry date** printed on it. Condoms are made of latex which can deteriorate with age so old ones are not safe.

Durex and some other condom brands are also individually **electronically tested**. This means every one's been stretched over a metal penis and had an electric current zapped through it. Rubber should act as a good insulator, so if any electricity leaks through, something's not right.

Also, just to be sure, Durex carry out random **air inflation tests** on batches of condoms. Normally they expect to be able to inflate individual condoms with up to 40 litres of air which is equivalent to nine gallons of water.

According to Durex, 50% of all women in Britain expect men to use condoms; 94% of people think it's

> *Lubricated condoms are safer than non-lubricated condoms because there's less friction and so less chance of splitting.*

responsible to use them; and 75% of under 20s see them as the best alternative to the Pill.

Fact

Nonoxynol-9 is a spermicide which is added to the lubricant on many condoms. Recent studies show that it contains good anti-viral properties and may even inactivate HIV on contact during sex.

GETTING INTO CONDOMS

The safest way to get into the foil wrapper of a condom is to just give it a careful rip between both sets of thumbs and forefingers. It's not a good idea to bite open wrappers, snip them open or rip them asunder, even if your passion is running near eruption point.

Condoms are made of thin latex rubber and easily rip on sharp fingernails, jewellery or teeth.

Once you've popped the rubber sheath out of its foil home, hold it flat so the bulblike teat end is sticking upwards. A few condoms brands don't have a teat. If that's the case, remember to leave about half an inch free at the top when you've put it on.

The bulb bit at the closed end, or the gap you leave if there's no bulb bit, is very important because this is where the spunk will gather when the penis ejaculates.

Squeeze the bulb between your thumb and forefinger to expel any air.

Hold the bulb of the condom at the tip of the penis and use the other hand to roll it down the length of the shaft.

> *Some people like to put a dab of water-based lubricant in the tip of condoms to help expel the air and give an extra smooth sensation during sex.*

A common mistake is to get the condom inside out. It won't unroll properly and will never reach the base of the penis. If it is inside out, pull it off, throw it away and start again.

During sex the condom can slip off if the penis loses some of its stiffness. It's a good precaution to keep checking occasionally to make sure it's still in place by feeling its position around the base of the penis.

After ejaculation, hold the condom in place as the penis is withdrawn. The penis might quickly go limp causing the condom to come loose. Holding it round the base of the penis keeps it on and stops any semen from escaping down the sides.

Never use a condom more than once.

After using condoms, wrap them in a tissue and put them in the bin.

Fact Over 140 million condoms are sold every year in the UK alone.

Practice makes perfect

The very worst time to learn how to fit a condom is a few seconds before you have sex for the first time. Think about it. When the chips are down and it's about to happen, your heart's beating like a drum, your hands are shaking, The last thing you want is to read the instruction slip in a pack of condoms. So practise. You could put one on when you wank. Practise single-handed – prepare for any eventualities.

If you're a woman, you could practise putting one on a banana, candle or anything penis-shaped.

Find out what condoms are like to handle so that when you reach that vital situation, you can focus all your attention on the good things going on and not have to worry about fitting a condom.

The things they say

Although condoms are a good contraceptive and the most effective barrier against infection, and although you can get them all over the place *still* some men get iffy about using them.

Men can come up with all manner of intriguing excuses as to why they shouldn't have to slip into a condom before sex. But if you're determined to use one and your prospective partner is trying to wriggle out, you definitely don't have to take no for an answer.

He says:	*'It's OK I'm clean'*
You say:	*'So are my windows. But I wouldn't have sex in front of them without drawing the curtains.'*
He says:	*'They're such horrible things'.*
You say:	*'So are pubs, mini cabs and fast food restaurants but it doesn't stop you slipping into them when the mood takes you.'*
He says:	*'Do I really have to have sex with you wearing a condom?'.*
You say:	*'Of course not. You could have sex without one on your own!'*
He says:	*'It won't feel like real sex if I wear one of those.'*
You say:	*'Well it won't feel like anything if you don't.'*

He says:	*'Wearing a condom might spoil my erection'.*
You say:	*'You worry about the condom, I'll take care of your erection.'*
He says:	*'If you really loved me you'd do it without one'.*
You say:	*'If you really loved me you'd respect the way I feel.'*
He says:	*'Condoms spoil the spontaneity of sex.'*
You say:	*'I'm more interested in sensuality than spontaneity.'*
He says:	*'Go on, please, can't we just do it without?'*
You say:	*'No!'*
He says:	*'Let me do it without one and I promise I won't come inside you'.*
You say:	*'Silly me, I thought Jackanory finished at 5 o'clock'.*
He says:	*'I can't bear anything to get in the way of our sex.'*
You say:	*'Well wear a condom and it won't'.*
He says:	*Without is so much better. You don't know what it feels like until you've tried it.*
You say:	*You could say the same for haemorrhoids.*

CONDOMS AND BOOZE

There's one thing that often gets in the way of people using condoms during sex: alcohol.

Getting drunk or stoned is cited as being the reason why a vast number of people who would normally use condoms, or definitely *want* to use condoms, don't.

> *"I admit I'm pathetic*
> *but I just don't think of condoms when I'm drunk."*
> (23 year old female)

The connection between getting drunk and not using condoms as only really been highlighted in recent years due to the incidence of HIV. But the connection between getting drunk and having sex has been recognised for a long time. Even in Shakespeare's day it was big news:

Macduff: What three things does drink especially provoke?

Porter: Marry sir, nose painting, sleep and urine. Lechery sir, it provokes and unprovokes; it provokes the desire, but it takes away the performance.

Macbeth

Drink and drugs are often associated with sex, partly because they're often the starting point for dating. Places that serve alcohol or where drugs are taken, like parties and clubs, are usually where people go to meet, often with a view to copping off together. So it's not surprising that the two go hand in hand.

> **"Sometimes you just don't have a Durex or you've had a drink. All you think is 'I've got a chance here for sex and if I don't take it now, I'll blow it'. So you go for it. I mean, it's hard work pulling in the first place."**
> (23 year old male)

But like Shakespeare says, it's the effect that intoxication has on the brain that can make the sex useless. Either through lost erections, sloppy behaviour, falling asleep at the wrong time or else doing it with someone you really wish you hadn't done it with, or doing something you really wish you hadn't done. Like having sex without a condom.

The fact is, alcohol might make you more frisky sexually. And it might lower your inhibitions socially, so you're more relaxed about talking to people you find attractive. But at the end of the day, it does no favours at all to your abilities under the duvet. It also does your capacity to choose who you do it with and how much care you take doing it, no good whatsoever.

LOVING LUBRICATION

Lubrication is a vital part of sex and it's an important part of safer sex. If sex was dry and scratchy it wouldn't be much fun at all. So the body naturally lubricates the vagina to make penetration more pleasurable. But not every woman's vagina produces sufficient lubrication all the time, sometimes it needs a little extra help.

And the anus has no natural lubricant like the vagina, so it definitely needs to have extra lubrication.

Safer sex with condoms is made safer still if extra lubrication is used. The more lubrication, the less friction. Friction is what normally causes rips and splits to appear in condoms.

Oil and rubber don't mix

Beware of oil-based lubricants when using condoms. The oil can very quickly rot the rubber in condoms, so when you're using them, don't use any oil-based brands like Vaseline or any other domestic oils like butter, margarine, coconut oil, cooking oil, massage oils or hand cream. Oil-based lubricants tend to trap germs more easily too because they're harder to clean off.

Water-based is best

The condom friendly lubricants to use are water-based lubricants. Water-based lubricants include:

- Senselle
- KY jelly
- Duragel
- Probe
- Ortho Lubricant
- Boots' own brand

Make sure lubricants are 'water-based' and not just

'water soluble'. The ones that are water soluble still have an oil base, it just means they'll wash out of sheets more easily.

Be lewd with lube

You don't have to be having penetrative sex to have fun with lubricants. Smearing some over the clitoris and vagina during masturbation adds to the sensual fluidity of the movements. And gently smoothing some over the head of an erect penis or pulling the foreskin back and forth over a squidge of jelly can be a rare old delight.

If you're going for a marathon stint of sex, lubrication will help you last longer without feeling a bit tender in intimate places.

Lubricants can be bought from pharmacists or from mail order catalogues specialising in sex aids.

Lube tube tips

Tubes of jelly can get very cold. You might want to squeeze a blob out and let it warm on your fingers before you touch your partner's tackle with it. Or who knows, you might find that the extra tingle from the cold sensation adds a few more degrees of pleasure.

Some lubricants don't taste too good. Try a few to find out if there's one that agrees with your taste buds.

KNOW YOUR CONDOM

Condoms come in a range of shapes colours, sizes and flavours: black ones, pink ones, thin ones, thick ones; there are strange ones with ribbing down the sides. Some are dry, some are wet. Some taste like a cool Caribbean rum punch, while others have a zingy smack of spearmint toothpaste.

But at the end of the day they all help to do the same job. They stop the passage of body fluids between you and your partner and minimize the chances of pregnancy or catching an infection. Remember to look for the kitemark as a mark of reliability (see page 91).

CONDOM SHOPPING

Recent risky times have made condoms potentially more and more important to everybody's sex life. And manufacturers aren't slow to grasp a good opportunity when it raises its head. So, they get down and get busy in the condom design department, trying to come up with a condom that will do the job, but which will also attract cash-waving punters. The result is a virtual smorgasbord of choice.

But sometimes you can be spoilt for choice. You just don't know which pack-of-three to toss in the shopping trolley and instead leave empty handed and confused.

To help, here's a quick once-round the rubber wear section:

WHAT'S ON OFFER

The different types of condoms on sale are:

ALLERGY. A few people find that condoms cause irritation. This can be caused by two things: spermicide or latex. Most reactions are caused by the spermicide that's used to lubricate them, which contains an ingredient called Nonoxynol-9. If you have a reaction swap to a condom like Durex Gossamer that doesn't contain a spermicide, just a lubricant like Sensitol. If you *still* experience irritation, you might possibly be allergic to the latex which is used to make condoms. So, the next move is to change to Durex Allergy, which not only doesn't contain Nonoxynol-9, but also has specially treated hypo-allergenic latex. For most people this change usually does the trick. If not, you might have a slight infection, so get checked out by your GP.

FLAVOURED. These can range in flavour from chocolate to banana, or from pina colada to strawberry daiquiri. Essentially they're flavoured to make oral sex more fun. As a rule, ordinary condoms don't taste too good. But sucking on a passion fruit flavoured, condom-clad penis might just be your idea of bliss!

Trying out a different flavour every night might add the ultimate taste sensation that your love life lacks. Who knows? Some flavoured brands don't carry the British Standards Institution Kitemark, so may not be strong enough for vaginal sex. None should be used for anal sex.

RIBBED. Ribbed condoms are basically the same as ordinary condoms, except that they have small raised rings around them that contour the shaft of the penis. The idea behind ribbed condoms like Durex Arouser or Ribbed Mates, is that the person being entered by a condom-wearing penis will gain an extra sexy sensation by the added tingle or friction of these bumps. Some people love them, others find them a bit too tickly and irritating.

EXTRA THIN. Men often complain that they don't like using condoms because they affect the quality of the sensations they feel. Some refuse to wear them because of lack of sensitivity. Condom manufacturers realise this and cleverly market brands like Durex Elite or Fetherlite, which are promoted as 'extra thin' to increase sensitivity. They can be very useful to persuade any reticent men to wear condoms, but they aren't necessarily suitable for very vigorous sex and definitely aren't strong enough for anal sex.

EXTRA STRONG. Certain sexual practices like anal sex require using a strong condom because there may well be a lot more friction and pressure brought to bear on the condom during intercourse. Often the anus is a tighter fit than a vagina and there isn't the same natural lubrication. So for anal sex, extra strong condoms like Durex Extra Strong or Superstrong Mates are preferable. But also, extra strong condoms make sense for all types of safer sex because they're less likely to split or tear.

EXTRA BIG. Condoms usually come in one-size-fits-all. And they do! No penis is too big for the average condom. But of course, the delicate macho ego doesn't like to believe this. And condoms manufacturers are very aware of the weaknesses of the male mind. They know all too well that if you call condoms Bigboy and Maxx, and claim they're a couple of inches bigger, then some men will be more than happy to buy them. Basically, extra big condoms are for extra big egos. However, some manufacturers are now making condoms in smaller sizes!

FEMALE CONDOM

You can now get condoms which fit inside a woman's vagina. Femidom is the only brand at the moment. They're made of soft polyurethane (like plastic) and work in the same way as the male condom.

Like the male condom, it takes a bit of practice to get used to using one. Here's how you do it:

- Hold the condom at the closed end and squeeze the inner ring between your thumb and middle finger. (It helps to keep your index finger on the inner ring to keep the condom steady.) Then put the squeezed ring into your vagina and push it up as far as it will go.
- Then put a finger inside the condom until you can feel the inner ring and push upwards until you can feel that it's lying just behind your pubic bone.
- Make sure that the outer ring and a small part of the sheath is lying closely against your vulva (the area just outside the vagina).

When you're having sex, guide the penis into the sheath, making sure that the penis doesn't go into your vagina *outside* the sheath. During sex, it will move about a bit but you'll be protected as long as the penis stays inside the sheath. After sex, and when you're ready, simply twist the outer ring to keep the semen inside and pull it out. Wrap in a tissue and put it in a bin.

BUYING CONDOMS

People get put off buying condoms. They feel embarrassed about going into a shop and saying "Can I have a packet of condoms please?", thinking that the person selling them is going to think "Aha, *that* customer is going to have sex some time soon." The truth is, they probably couldn't give a toss. They normally have better things on their minds – like "When am I going to get home to watch *Blind Date*/ eat my dinner/play strip Scrabble/have sex?".

You could always try the faceless approach of a supermarket and bury a packet of three in a basket of groceries. Or, if the difficulty of buying them is going to stop you using them, you could use a vending machine or mail order. You can get them free from: family planning clinics; GUM clinics and Brook Advisory Centres.

Chapter 7

Pregnancy

❝ In the end it's your choice.
But sometimes it helps to talk
it over with other people. ❞

23 year old
female

You've missed a period, your breasts are swollen and tender, you're feeling tired and drained … You think you're pregnant and you want to find out as soon as possible.

PREGNANCY TESTS

Pregnancy tests can be carried out on a sample of urine from the first day of a missed period. There are different ways of confirming you're pregnant. Your choices are:

- *home tests* – available from most pharmacists, these doityourself kits are quick and convenient. Most will give you a result within 30 minutes. They cost between £6 and £10, but at least you're the first to know.
- *pharmacist's tests* – you can take a urine sample into a pharmacist for testing and get a result in as little as five minutes. Costs around £5.
- *family planning clinic* – some FPAs offer free tests with results within minutes.
- *your GP* – who may test your sample on the spot or send it away to a lab.

Whatever you choose to do, the result might come as a shock. If you're pregnant, maybe you'll be delighted, maybe you'll be totally panicked, or maybe you'll just be stunned. Whatever the result, you'll need to work out what you think and feel about the outcome. Talk it through with people you trust; friends or relatives. Or talk to the baby's father. Don't try to deal with the situation entirely on your own.

VISIT YOUR GP

Whether or not you've had a pregnancy test, go and see your GP as soon as you think you're pregnant. The earlier you do it the better, because it's through your GP that you can make arrangements for antenatal care (the care you'll get leading up to the birth of your baby) and your baby's birth. He or she will explain what will happen in the next few weeks and make an appointment for you to visit an antenatal clinic. You'll need to think about a lot of things, including where to have your baby, how to keep healthy in your pregnancy, making arrangements for work, sorting out your rights and benefits, etc.

UNHAPPY ABOUT BEING PREGNANT

Pregnancy isn't always good news. If you never intended to get pregnant, but it happened, then the reality can be very upsetting. For your own sake, it's important to act fairly quickly and come to a decision about whether or not you want to have an abortion. It definitely helps to talk this through with someone.

Once arranged, abortions are performed safely, swiftly and within the law. But making the necessary arrangements takes time so it's *vital* to act as soon as you think you're pregnant, and as soon as you're *sure* abortion is the right choice for you.

The earlier you have the abortion, the better. Strictly

speaking, abortions are legal up to 24 weeks of pregnancy, but doctors don't like performing them this late and it can also be far more traumatic for you. Most abortions are performed within the first 12 weeks of pregnancy that's 12 weeks from the start of your last period, because they're easier and safer. Don't risk waiting until you've missed a second period.

Abortion procedure

Two doctors must agree that a woman's, or her family's, physical or mental health will be threatened if she continues with the pregnancy. If you want a free abortion on the NHS, your GP will have to agree and refer you to a hospital. They have a legal duty to give you confidential advice and make the appropriate referral. But as some don't agree with abortion, attitudes and actions vary. Your GP may be sympathetic or you may be told that an NHS abortion is difficult because of health waiting lists.

Private alternatives

Some women immediately choose to go privately, because it's easier and quicker to arrange an abortion this way, plus they're carried out in a sympathetic atmosphere. But of course it can cost between £200 and £500.

If you do choose to go private your best bet is to contact one of the charitable organisations like the British Pregnancy Advisory Service (BPAS), the Pregnancy Advisory Service (PAS) or the Marie Stopes Clinics who are very supportive and try to keep costs low. Alternatively, under 26s can contact the Brook Advisory Centre in London for advice and referral to one of the above, or if possible, an NHS hospital.

What happens next

Whatever organisation you end up going to NHS, private or charity clinic the procedure's roughly the same. Your pregnancy will be confirmed, then you'll see the first doctor who'll examine you before asking about your situation and medical history. You'll be asked why you want an abortion and if you've considered the alternatives. If they agree an abortion is appropriate, they'll sign an authorising form.

You'll see the second doctor immediately if you're at a charity or private clinic. For an NHS abortion you'll probably be referred to a hospital. Once the second doctor has given their authorisation an appointment for the operation is made, as soon as possible. If you haven't heard by the time you're near your 12th week of pregnancy, contact the doctor immediately.

WHERE TO GO

Addresses and contacts of organisations who help with pregnancy testing, abortion, information and counselling are listed on page 138.

Chapter 8

Sexual problems

❝ *Don't believe any man who says he's never had a problem getting it up — it happens to us all at one time or another.* **❞**

27 year old male

EXPECTATIONS

Because sex is a complicated relationship between two people, things can go wrong. And one downside of the way sex is portrayed in films and romantic novels is that we grow up with unrealistic expectations of sex.

Many magazines for both women and men pedal an unreasonable range of expectations about multi-orgasmic sexual experiences. Part of the problem is that many readers then start to feel inadequate about their own real-life sexual experiences.

There are a few sexual problems that can occur between partners and with individuals. But on the whole sex for the majority of us is mostly good, occasionally great and just an alright, cosy, gently satisfying experience, the rest of the time.

We all have a right to enjoy sex. None of us should have to do anything we don't want to. We shouldn't be embarrassed about our needs and desires and it's perfectly natural to talk through sexual fantasies with a lover. Sex is just sex. We're not talking earth tremors under the duvet that register on the Richter Scale.

The more realistic our expectations, the more honest we get about our fears and the more adaptable and responsive we become to our lovers, the more sex can become an enjoyable and enhancing part of life.

COMMON PROBLEMS

There are certain problems which can affect lovers, both men and women, and spoil sex.

Nerves

Trying to have sex while you're too anxious or too nervous about your partner or the situation where you're having sex can be bad news. The best sex is the stuff where you can relax into what you're doing, totally lose yourself in a mood of sensual feeling and excitement. This isn't easy if you're worrying about:

- getting pregnant
- catching an STD
- being interrupted in the height of passion
- doing something your lover doesn't like
- having smelly breath/feet/genitals/armpits
- knowing you'll regret it all the next day

Arousal

Nerves can badly affect arousal too. Arousal is very important when it comes to sex. If a woman isn't sufficiently aroused then she won't relax and the chances are her vagina won't lubricate itself and become moist. A dry vagina can make any attempt to have sex or even be penetrated by a lover's finger, very uncomfortable. Similarly, if a man isn't sexually aroused, then his penis won't become erect.

We can be aroused by either physical stimulation;

being touched, stroked and kissed and/or by mental stimulation; sexy thoughts or a sexy atmosphere. If you don't feel like sex or something puts you off, then it's very hard to get aroused. If you're not aroused, you won't enjoy, or maybe won't even be able to have, sex.

Turn offs

Worry, pain, fear, pressure or just plain fatigue can all be a turn off to sex. If you've got something more important on your mind that won't go away, if you feel pressured into 'performing' sexually, if you're scared of your partner, or scared of getting caught, or if something hurts any of these can dampen your ardour.

Sharp nails, dirty hands, being too rough, playing dead, making too much noise all or any of these things might put you or your partner off. But none of them are insurmountable. A bit of chat and honesty can put a lot of sex problems to rest.

COMMON FEMALE PROBLEMS

Pain or dryness during penetration

Reasons: Taking things too quickly and not allowing the vagina to get sufficiently lubricated naturally, before trying to put in the penis. If it's first-time sex, then the hymen (the membrane across the entrance to the vagina) might not have been broken. Some women do feel uncomfortable sensations from having a penis too deep inside of them.

Cures: The best treatment for dryness is lots of prepenetration attention. Lots of hugging, kissing and stroking. It might help to use a lubricant inside the vagina too. Something like KY jelly can help reach the parts that otherwise remain dry. Before penetration it helps to smear some lubricant on the tip of the penis too. If the hymen's unbroken then gradual and gentle penetration will help stretch and break it. Lots of lubricant, gentle pushes and patience are the key. For penetration that feels too deep for comfort, the best cure is for the woman to sit on top. That way she can guide the penis inside her and so control the depth of penetration herself.

"KY jelly is the answer. It makes everything sort of silky and squishy. Like a banana and custard."
(19 year old female)

Penis has trouble entering the vagina

Reason: Some women's vaginas go into spasm and close up. This is a medical condition known as vaginismus. As with many sexual problems, a cycle can occur where because there's a problem with sex, every time you get near having it, you get upset and uptight, which makes the problem worse.

Cure: Learning to relax and feel comfortable with sex and penetration. Exercises include breathing control and very gradual insertion of your own finger inside your vagina. This can be done using a warm bath to help you relax. In time it's possible to learn to relax the muscle at will.

Can't reach an orgasm

Reasons: We're all individual. Some women reach orgasm every time they masturbate or have sex. Some women never have orgasms. Too much pressure from a lover to have one can put you off. People can't just 'give' you orgasms. You need to learn how to get there yourself. Even the greatest lover in the world would be useless to you if you haven't learnt how to relax and have an orgasm. Some women try too hard to have an orgasm and stop themselves from just relaxing. Others don't have them because they can't deal with the emotional feeling of letting go and being out of control. Some women associate sex with guilt. Others may be too physically self conscious to enjoy the feelings of sex.

Cure: Explore your own body and learn to masturbate. Experiment somewhere warm and safe. Touch your nipples, your clitoris, your vagina. Do whatever feels nice. Concentrate on the sensations. Carry on, but don't set your sights on orgasm. If you find yourself getting more aroused, speed up the

"The first time I ever came was when my boyfriend masturbated me with his hand. The first time it was quite mild. Now I've had four or five and it gets better and better."
(19 year old female)

rhythm of touching, maybe push your fingers inside your vagina. Stop whenever you want to. The more you experiment and the more you practise, the more likely you are to find out what gets you going and what makes you come. The joy is, once you've found out for yourself, you can then show your lover what to do for you.

COMMON MALE PROBLEMS

Pain with erections or intercourse

Reasons: A tight foreskin can cause pain during erection and intercourse.

Cure: Pulling the foreskin backwards and forwards with soap and water or even KY jelly to lubricate it might help. The foreskin can be loosened by a simple surgical operation, or in severe cases circumcision might be necessary.

Coming too quickly

Reasons: Normally caused by natural sexual stimulation, premature ejaculation happens to every man at least once, and usually lots of times. Even the most experienced lovers might come really quickly on their first time with a new partner or when they're especially excited. Premature ejaculation's another one of those problems that can set up a vicious circle where you come quickly once, then worry so much that it's going to happen on another occasion that your anxiety triggers it off.

Cure: Men can learn to control their ejaculation. The simplest way is to practise while masturbating. Stimulate yourself until you are just about to come, then stop. Think about something really unsexy, a massive turn off, like John Major's socks, train spotting in Crewe, the Dow Jones index – anything. Hold the horrible thought, don't touch yourself and wait a minute or two until your erection is beginning to wilt, then start again. Do the same thing, almost come, then stop. After three or four dry runs, let yourself come. Practise this a few times a week and you'll eventually gain control of your orgasm. The same thing can be done during sex, with your partner's help. Try moving your penis inside your partner until you're about to come, then stop. Think unsexy thoughts, let the come feeling pass, then start again. Keep doing it until you can sustain longer periods without wanting to come.

> *"Masturbation was the key. Learning to come, or rather not to come, to order makes such a difference."*
> (23 year old male)

Keeping an erection

Reasons: Nerves, fatigue, booze and drugs can all have a very detrimental affect on a stiffy. Occasional bouts of impotence are perfectly normal and will often pass of their own accord. Getting too anxious and upset about the problem usually only worsens the situation.

Cure: Trying too hard to have sex when you're having erection problems can make things worse. The best thing to do is to agree with your partner that for a while you'll have a pact not to try penetration. Instead, concentrate on exploring each other's bodies, trying out massage, licking, touching,

"It's taken me ages to relax with a girl. After a couple of failed attempts, all I could think about when I was with a girl was my erection. All my thoughts were focused on my penis. I'd close my eyes and try to keep it stiff. I was going about it all wrong. I was so scared of failure, I made myself fail."
(25 year old male)

nuzzling, then having loads of cuddles and soft words. For the first few times, even if you do get an erection, don't try to have sex or even masturbate each other. After a few times move to touching each others' genital areas. Eventually stage by stage reach the point where the penis is put inside your lover, but just hold it there, kissing and talking and stroking, don't feel pressure to perform. In time as you both become comfortable with not trying to achieve sexual goals but just enjoying each other's bodies, the ability to gain and sustain and erection should become easier.

Fact **International cures for impotence include:** crocodile kidneys (Australia), sea slugs (West Indies), snakeburger (Japan), rattlesnake (USA) or celery (Norway)

A PROBLEM THAT ISN'T A PROBLEM

We never seem to come at exactly the same time

Reason: Simultaneous orgasm is a very rare thing. Again, Hollywood movies have a lot to answer for in this respect. Most women need to have some clitoral stimulation before or after penetration to reach a climax. Just having a penis inside them doesn't mean the fireworks are guaranteed by any means.

Cure: There isn't one and you'd be doing your sex life no favours trying to achieve one. Sex is about giving and receiving pleasure. One of the most intensely pleasurable things about having sex with another person is enjoying seeing them getting off on what you're doing. It's a real bonus when you get to see and feel them come too. But you're too busy trying to come yourself at the same time, you miss out on the fun. The same is true in reverse, if you get too obsessed with making them come, you miss out on the pleasure they're giving you.

WHERE YOU CAN GET HELP...

If you've got a sexual problem that you'd like to talk through with a professional, you can go to your GP and ask to be referred to a psychosexual counsellor or a clinic. Or you can go to Relate, a family planning clinic or else get in touch with the British Association of Counselling and ask for the contact of a suitable counsellor.

Sexual problems are often the last sort of problems that people deal with in their lives because they feel an embarrassment about them, purely because they relate to a taboo subject. But with most other life problems, the longer you leave things and the more secretive you are about them, the worse they can get.

Honesty with yourself is the first step, admitting that something isn't quite right. Honesty with your partner is just as important if it involves them. Seeking out as much information as you can is a good move. There are loads of books on the subject. Maybe lastly, if things don't get better quickly, you can get the advice of a trained professional.

"Going to sex therapist was one of the most embarrassing moments of my life – but it turned out to be the best thing I ever did. I think my wife would agree too."
(25 year old male)

Chapter 9

Sexually transmitted diseases

" Until you know someone who's caught something you don't think about it, do you? It's real but it's not the sort of thing that happens to us. "

21 year old male

The fact is, if you're having sex, you could easily catch a sexually transmitted disease (STD). You don't have to be promiscuous to get an STD. *Anyone* can get one – straight, gay, lesbian, bisexual, male, female. STDs are an equal opportunities affliction, they're totally non-racist, non-sexist, non-classist and non-ageist in who they choose to infect. They're equally available to everyone.

Just because STDs are very common and relatively easy to get hold of, doesn't mean you won't feel embarrassed and even guilty that you've got one. But whatever you do, don't let this stop you from seeking proper medical help.

> *"The first time I went to a clinic I thought I ought to wear a balaclava and dark glasses so as no one would clock me. But after a couple of visits it was easy. I used to just sit there and get a kick out of watching other guys coming in for the first time and looking all sheepish like I did."*
> (25 year old male)

There are several common STDs and many have very similar symptoms. It's almost impossible to diagnose and treat yourself; which is why it's vital to make an appointment with a special (GUM, STD) clinic without delay, if something's feeling a bit iffy.

THINGS TO WATCH OUT FOR

WOMEN
● a change in your vaginal secretions (discharge).

MEN
● discharge from the penis
● itching/discharge from the anus

MEN AND WOMEN
● pain or stinging when you urinate
● a burning feeling around your genital area
● blisters, lumps, ulcers or sores on or near the genitals
● itching in your pubic hair

You should go for a check up if: you have any of these symptoms; a partner tells you that he or she has an STD; or a cervical smear test shows that you have an infection of some kind.

Some STDs don't have any symptoms so you may only find out that you have one if a partner tells you that he or she has an STD. If this happens, you must get checked out yourself.

Sometimes STDs can appear when you have a new partner but not always. The germ can be inside you without giving you any problems. So it's not always a sign of infidelity if you or your partner suddenly develop symptoms of an STD.

IF YOU THINK YOU'VE GOT AN STD...

See your GP

He or she may be able to help you. If not, you'll be referred to a special clinic, also called GUM (genito-urinary medicine), or STD clinic. These clinics specialise in STDs and the service and treatment is free and confidential. Once there, you'll have the necessary tests, have all your questions about your STD answered and get the treatment you need.

Finding your nearest clinic

- look in the phone book under 'genito-urinary medicine', STD or VD, or
- phone your local hospital and ask for the special clinic, or
- contact the Family Planning Association (071-636 7866) and ask for Clinic Enquiries Service, or
- ring the National AIDS Helpline (0800-567 123), a free, anonymous, 24-hour phoneline, that can give you the number and address of your local clinic.

"I felt like a leper having to go to a special clinic. I told my best friend, to see if she'd come with me. It was only then I found out she'd already been and so had two other friends. It was no big deal. Like going to the doctor's really, only the magazines in the waiting room weren't so old!"

(21 year old female)

How to tell your partner(s)

If you find out you've got an STD, it's a considerate and responsible act, to tell the person or people you've recently slept with. Then they should go for a check-up too. Of course, informing someone that you may have passed on a disease to them isn't a very pleasant prospect. But try to remember that STDs are very commonplace. So you're not alone. It doesn't mean you're guilty, bad or evil. Don't try to find anyone to blame. Looking for blame is pointless, the best thing is just to deal with the disease. Deal with it as quickly as possible and help to stop the infection spreading and making anyone else suffer a hard time.

Instead of thinking that you're going to be telling your partners some awful news, look upon it as doing for their own benefit. You're being responsible and caring by being honest. If you're worried about telling, ask for advice when you visit the special clinic.

Long-term relationships

Honesty is usually the best policy in these matters. If you've got an infection by having sex outside the relationship and there's a good chance that you've passed it on to your long-term partner, trying to lie will do your relationship no favours. Your partner will put two and two together anyway, and if you then lie to their questions, it's an insult to them and your trust. If you lie and get away with it, there's a very good chance they'll never quite be sure of you again. If you tell the truth, it's a lot easier to live with yourself and at least you're giving them the opportunity to decide how they want to proceed. If you lie, you're endangering their well-being too.

Don't have sex

If you think you've got an STD, don't have sex until you've had a check-up, completed treatment and got the all-clear. If you're in a long-term relationship and don't usually use condoms, keep using them for at least three months after treatment. You could re-infect each other. Otherwise, use condoms at all times.

Be condom clever

Using condoms and practising safer sex can greatly reduce your chances of catching most of the diseases that are transmitted through sex. Condoms are an easy and effective way of protecting you and your sexual partners from a lot of itching, weeping, worrying and trips to the clinic.

HIV AND AIDS

"Good Christian people who would not dream of misbehaving will not catch AIDS."
Edwina Currie, *Guardian*
(13 Feb 87)

True, if good Christian people never have sex or are totally 100 per cent monogamous with an HIV-free partner, they will not get AIDS. But some good Christian people do have sex and many are not monogamous. And they, good Christians or not, are at just as much risk as the rest of the non-celibate community.

What is it? HIV is a virus which attacks your body's immune system and can lead to AIDS. AIDS is an immunity disorder, which means your body loses it's natural ability to fight diseases. In many cases, sufferers die from diseases like pneumonia, which would normally not be fatal if the body was fit. HIV leads to AIDS in the majority of cases.

How do I know if I've got it? There are no symptoms of HIV and you won't know whether you're carrying HIV antibodies until you have a special HIV antibody test. So you can't tell whether somebody has HIV just by looking. This is why practising safer sex is so important.

How can I get it? Semen, blood, saliva and vaginal juices are all body fluids which can contain HIV. They're also body fluids which are commonly exchanged during unprotected sex. Vaginal, anal and oral sex without a condom can all lead to the passing on HIV, if one of the partners is carrying the virus.

HIV can also be passed from one drug user to another by sharing needles or works. So don't share works.

A mother can pass the virus to her baby, either in the womb, during birth or through breast-feeding.

In rare instances, if the equipment hasn't been sterilised, you can become infected through having a tattoo, acupuncture, ear-piercing or electrolysis. So always choose a reliable practitioner.

You can't get HIV via blood transfusions in Britain because all blood has been checked for HIV since 1985, but you do run the risk of contracting it if you have a transfusion in some other countries.

What can I do about it? The only way to know definitely whether you have HIV is to have a blood test for HIV antibodies. These are what your blood creates to try and combat the virus. Think very carefully before having a test. It's important to talk to a health adviser at a special clinic before having the test as there are many things to be taken into consideration.

Preparing for the test

Having a test is a big decision. It's not one to be taken lightly. Knowing that you definitely have the virus can have a major effect on your life. It could influence your whole future plans, make you radically change the way you behave or cause you to feel immense depression or shock. On the other hand, having a test and finding out that no HIV antibodies are present, can lead some people to believe they're untouchable. They might think they can go on taking risks and always get away with it.

Reasons to be tested

- If you're uncomfortably worried that you might have the virus and not knowing the truth badly affects your life.
- You're ill and the doctor thinks it might be HIV-related. Knowing for sure means you could get suitable treatment.
- You reasonably think you might have HIV and by knowing you can get treatment to avoid catching illnesses associated with the virus.

The test

If you decide to go have the test, you can get it done at a special clinic or at your GP surgery.

- You'll be asked questions about your sex life over the last six months.
- A small sample of blood is taken from your arm.
- You get the results from one day to four weeks after the test is carried out.
- Whether the result is positive or negative, you should continue counselling with a health adviser. If you need advice or information about the test, phone the National AIDS Helpline 0800-567 123.

What's the treatment? There are drugs available which slow down the progression of the disease and prevent other infections, but there's no real cure as yet.

 **OR**

False: You can only catch HIV or STDs if the male ejaculates.

True: Most males have some pre-ejaculation cum which can easily contain the virus, and any cuts or sores on the penis could be enough to pass on infection.

False: Oral sex is more risky for catching HIV than any other type of sex.

True: Oral sex is actually likely to be safer than vaginal sex or anal sex.

False: You can catch HIV from kissing.

True: There is no evidence to prove that HIV has ever been transmitted by kissing.

False: You can catch HIV from toilet seats.

True: The virus is actually very weak and can't live outside the body. It has to be passed in blood or body fluids.

False: The Pill protects you against catching HIV.

True: The Pill is an effective contraceptive, but if you have sex without condoms, you're still mixing body fluids. Body fluids carry the virus.

False: You can catch HIV from drinking the water in Africa.

True: HIV can only live in blood and body fluids. It can't survive outside the body.

False: AIDS is a gay disease.

True: Heterosexuals and bisexuals are just as likely to be infected by the virus if they have sex with an infected partner. The biggest percentage rise in new cases last year was among heterosexuals.

False: Only heroin addicts or people who've had blood transfusions get HIV and AIDS.

True: Anyone who mixes blood or body fluids with an infected person can get HIV.

YOU'VE READ THE BOOK, NOW …

Good sex takes time and effort. A spot of 'wham-bang-thank-you-mam!' isn't going to light anyone's fire. Good sex is about caring, understanding and exciting your partner as well as yourself.

But that doesn't mean it's easy. In Hollywood sex, two practical strangers can melt into each other's arms, stylishly divest their designer togs and within seconds be engulfed in a choreographed ballet of beautiful bodies emitting life-changing, earth trembling ooohs and aaahs, as they glide towards orgasmic nirvana. In real life it just doesn't happen like that – not all the time!

Even when you've known someone for years, been great friends, love them dearly and fancy their pants off, still the sex can be tricky, confusing or just plain disappointing.

Sex is a bit like dancing or figure skating. The first time round with a new partner, you'll spend most of your time with one eye watching what they do, trying to work out where to put you hands and feet, on what beat. And chances are it'll all end up being a bit of a dog's dinner. Fair enough. Next time out it'll get better as you predict their steps and throw in a few of your own. With a bit of luck, after a few rehearsals you'll make Torvill and Dean look like rank amateurs.

USEFUL ADDRESSES

Counselling

British Association for Counselling
37A Sheep Street, Rugby, Warwickshire CV21 3BX
Tel: (0788) 578 328
For sympathetic and impartial counselling on personal, emotional, sexual, family and other problem.

AIDS

National AIDS Helpline – (0800) 567 123
Confidential 24-hour helpline for anyone with questions on HIV or AIDS. Calls are free and not itemised on bills.
Minicom terminal for hard of hearing:
(0800) 521 361 (10am-10pm)
Bengali, Gujarati, Hindi, Punjabi, Urdu:
(0800) 282 445 (Wed 6pm-10pm)
Cantonese: (0800) 282 446 (Tues 6pm-10pm)
Arabic: (0800) 282 447 (Wed 6pm-10pm)

Body Positive
51B Philbeach Gardens, London SW5 9EB
Heipline: (071) 373 9124
Self-help and support groups for people affected by HIV.

Positively Women
5 Sebastian St, London EC1V 0HE
Tel: (071) 490 5515 (Mon-Fri 10am-4pm. Tues 10am-2pm)
Women offering support, counselling and information to women with HIV and AIDS.
Helpline: (071) 490 2327 (Mon-Fri 12am-2pm)

Terrence Higgins Trust
52-54 Grays Inn Road, London WC1X 8JU
Helpline: (071) 242 1010 (3pm-10pm)
Legal line: (071) 405 2381 (Wed 7pm-10pm)
Information, advice and help on HIV and AIDS.

Family planning, pregnancy advice and abortion

British Pregnancy Advisory Service (BPAS)
Austy Manor, Wootton Wawen, Solihull, West Midlands B95 6BX
Tel: (0564) 793 225
Advice and counselling on pregnancy (including unwanted pregnancy and abortion), infertility, sexual problems and sterilisation.

Family Planning Association
27-35 Mortimer St, London W1N 7JR
Tel: (071) 636 7866
Information on all FP clinics in the UK as well as all aspects of family planning and sexual health.

Marie Stopes House
The Well Woman Centre, 108 Whitfield St, London W1P 9JP
Tel: (071) 388 0662/2585 Mon-Wed 9am-8pm.
Thurs, Fri, Sat 9am-5pm.
Counselling and information on women's sexual health, including contraception and pregnancy. Branches in Leeds and Manchester.

Maternity Alliance
15 Britannia St, London WC1 9JP
Tel: (071) 837 1265
Advice on rights and benefits during pregnancy and after the birth.

Gay and lesbian

Lesbian and Gay Switchboard
BM Switchboard, London WC1N 3XX
Tel: (071) 837 7324
24-hour information and helpline. Other switchboards operate all over the country, look in local press for details or ring London switchboard and ask for your local number.

Health

Health Education Authority
Hamilton House, Mabledon Place, London WC1H 9TX
Tel: (071) 383 3833

For leaflets and books on a range of health topics.
Scotland: Health Education Board for Scotland (031) 447 8044
Wales: Health Promotion Wales (0222) 752 222
Northern Ireland: Health Promotion Agency
Northern Ireland (0232) 311 611

Rape

Rape Crisis Centres
PO Box 69, London WC1X 9NJ
Tel: (071) 837 1600
Confidential counselling for rape victims. Volunteers may be able
to accompany you to report incident to the police. Branches in
London, Belfast, Cardiff, Dublin and Edinburgh.

Rape Helplines
Belfast: (0232) 249 696
Cardiff: (0222) 373 181
Cork: (010) 35321 968086
Dublin: (010) 35331 661 4911/661 4564
Dundee: (0382) 201 291
Edinburgh: (031) 556 9437
Strathclyde: (041) 221 8448

Relationship and sexual problems

Brook Advisory Centres
153A East Street, London SE17 2SD
Tel: (071) 708 1234
Counselling to young people with relationship and sexual
problems as well as family planning advice and help with
unwanted pregnancies. Phone for details of your nearest centre.
Helpline: (071) 617 800
National 24-hour helpline offering advice and information.

Relate (National Marriage Guidance Council)
Herbert Gray College, Little Church St,
Rugby CV21 3AP
Tel: (0788) 573 241
Counselling for individuals or couples, married or single, with
relationship problems.

PENGUIN BOOKS

Published by the Penguin Group
Penguin Books Ltd, 27 Wrights Lane, London W8 5TZ, England
Penguin Books USA Inc., 375 Hudson Street, New York, New York 10014, USA
Penguin Books Australia Ltd, Ringwood, Victoria, Australia
Penguin Books Canada Ltd, 10 Alcorn Avenue, Toronto, Ontario, Canada M4V 3B
Penguin Books (NZ) Ltd, 182–190 Wairau Road, Auckland 10, New Zealand

Penguin Books Ltd, Registered Offices: Harmondsworth, Middlesex, England

Commissioned and developed by the Health Education Authority
Published in Penguin Books 1994
10 9 8 7 6 5 4 3 2 1

Typeset by Type Generation, London

Printed in England by Clays Ltd, St Ives plc